Governing Soviet Cities

William Taubman

Sponsored by
The Russian Institute of
Columbia University

The Praeger Special Studies program—
utilizing the most modern and efficient book
production techniques and a selective
worldwide distribution network—makes
available to the academic, government, and
business communities significant, timely
research in U.S. and international economic, social, and political development.

Governing Soviet Cities
Bureaucratic Politics and Urban Development in the USSR

Praeger Publishers New York Washington London

PRAEGER SPECIAL STUDIES IN INTERNATIONAL ECONOMICS AND DEVELOPMENT

Library of Congress Cataloging in Publication Data

Taubman, William
    Governing Soviet cities.

    (Praeger special studies in international
economics and development)
    "Sponsored by the Russian Institute of Columbia
University."
    Bibliography: p.
    1. Municipal government—Russia. I. Columbia
University. Russian Institute. II. Title.
JS6058. T36   320. 4   72-92474

PRAEGER PUBLISHERS
111 Fourth Avenue, New York, N.Y. 10003, U.S.A.
5, Cromwell Place, London S.W.7, England

Published in the United States of America in 1973
by Praeger Publishers, Inc.

Printed in the United States of America

To Jane

Some years ago, when I was in residence in Moscow State University as an exchange student doing research on Soviet cities, an article in a Soviet journal by the mayor of a small Soviet city caught my eye.

"It has become common to hail the city soviet as master of the city," wrote the mayor of Chervonograd, a city of more than 50,000 in Lvov Province in the Ukraine. He continued:

> That is a healthy thought and so it should be. The rights of city soviets are clearly defined in the Fundamental Law—the USSR Constitution. . . . But unfortunately, far from all city soviets are able to utilize these powers. In fact, as a general rule, the local economy is not in their hands, but is scattered among various agencies. Much has been said and written against this arrangement, but so far without having any effect. Relations between soviets and these agencies are not defined. That is why soviets must often play the role of suppliants and not organs of state power. That is the cause, in our opinion, of all the trouble.[1]

"All the trouble" in Chervonograd, a coal-mining center founded in 1951, consisted of unbalanced urban development, with industrial expansion outstripping the supply of housing and municipal services. The city government (city soviet) was responsible for balanced development, but could neither carry out its mandate nor prevent industrial enterprises from doing as they pleased.

I noted down the details of the mayor's comment. Almost all the city's housing belonged to a coal trust, Chervonograd Coal, which took care of its own workers but was reluctant to grant space to "aliens"—to medical personnel, schoolteachers, workers in clothing and stocking factories and service establishments. Not even in its own houses was the city sovereign, since these received water and heat from the trust. Every street was a potential source of confusion and acrimony, for, although the streets and sidewalks were maintained by the city, all water and sewage pipes and electrical lines were the trust's. One could expect the trust to supply its own people with balanced housing and services, but according to the mayor, "All they care about is chalking up square meters. They don't even care if no grass grows around the houses."

Chervonograd's problems were aggravated, concluded its mayor, by the fragmentation of authority among a variety of agencies. "To our city more than to any other the old proverb applies: With seven nannies the child loses an eye."

Was Chervonograd, as its mayor claimed, an extreme case? Or did it exemplify a syndrome that takes different forms in different cities but obeys the same principle in all—What's Good for Chervonograd Coal is Good for Chervonograd? Who governs Soviet cities? How? And with what results? Needless to say, these are official questions. My attempt at answers is in this book.

I had as many opportunities as I might have wished to see Soviet city politics in action. I did, however, have opportunities for which I am grateful. I read Soviet kandidat and doctoral dissertations in Lenin Library. I read local newspapers, and gathered books and pamphlets issued in small editions and hence unavailable in the United States. I talked with Soviet professors of law and government, as well as with some city officials.[2]

Lack of biographical information has hampered many areas of Soviet studies. But while more data has become available on central, republic, and province leaders, it remains difficult if not impossible to discover who's who in many cities. When names are available, information about officials' background is lacking. And even when one knows something about past career and present prestige, one cannot be sure what weight to assign these factors in estimating political influence.[3]

The role of the Communist Party presents special problems. According to Party Rules, city Party committees should play perhaps the decisive role in urban governance. In some cases they do. But in other cities, in similar cases, the Party is not mentioned. Are some Party leaders guilty of politically motivated false modesty? Their problem is that the Party Rules say they must "lead" the municipal government but neither "supplant" it nor permit "a merging of functions" with city authorities.[4] City Party leaders must wish to appear as benevolent tutors; city officials depict themselves as effective without Party aid. Both preferences may combine with the Party's general unwillingness to disclose the details of its activities to produce vague and inconsistent reports of its role.

The possibility of false modesty on the part of Party leaders raises the question of the veracity of other information. Some journalists and scholars have been both reporters of the status quo and advocates of reforms to strengthen city governments. Their testimony is crucial, but is it fair? Of all periodicals examined, Izvestiia and Sovety deputatov trudiashchikhsia have published the most articles on city problems, and those most sympathetic to the "urban cause." But neither has been an uncritical ally. Both have unmasked lax city officials as well as endorsed efficient ones; while calling for change, both have been careful also to urge that city leaders better employ the powers they have.

Can we credit the word of city leaders themselves? One is reassured by the internal consistency among accounts of similar problems in different cities, and by agreement among different reports on particular cities. (Where two accounts conflict, both are mentioned.) One notes further that those whom city officials attack do not generally deny the charges (some are too busy ignoring them), nor do most city leaders plead innocent (although many cite extenuating circumstances) to indictments levelled against them.

The whole truth and nothing but the truth? Rather, in this book, the truth as I have been able to glean it. To the extent I have succeeded I owe thanks to a number of individuals and institutions. While at Columbia University I had important help from Professor John Hazard, who guided my dissertation and first turned me toward the topic, and from Professor Peter Juviler, who offered constructive criticism. At a later stage the manuscript was read by Jerry F. Hough of Toronto University and Earl Latham of Amherst College. That my approach to Soviet urban government and Professor Hough's have turned out to move in parallel is reassuring indeed, and so I hasten to return the compliments he has offered me elsewhere and to acknowledge that his advice is reflected in several places in this book, particularly the last chapter. To Professor Latham my thanks are given not only for his criticism but for his friendship.

Along the way several organizations have provided financial and logistical assistance. Work related to this book began and proceeded with help from the Foreign Area Fellowship Program. Later the Inter-University Committee on Travel Grants made it possible for me to spend a year in Moscow, while a Fulbright-Hays Fellowship paid my way. Needless to say neither these organizations nor any individuals are responsible for any errors that remain.

CONTENTS

LIST OF TABLES

ABBREVIATIONS OF JOURNAL AND BOOK TITLES

Bulletin-Moscow: Biulleten' Ispolnitel'nogo Komiteta Moskovskogo Gorodskogo Soveta Deputatov Trudiashchikhsia.

CDSP: Current Digest of the Soviet Press.

Plenum CC: Plenum Tsentral'nogo Komiteta Kommunisticheskoi Partii Sovetskogo Soiuza: stenograficheskii otchet (Plenum of the Central Committee of the Communist Party of the Soviet Union: stenographic report). Moscow: Gosudarstvennoe Izdatel'stvo Politicheskoi Literatury. [Citations in footnotes include dates of specific plenums. Complete information, including publication date, is in the Bibliography.]

RSFSR Zasedaniia: Zasedaniia Verkhovnogo Soveta RSFSR: stenograficheskii otchet (Meetings of the RSFSR Supreme Soviet: stenographic report). Moscow. [Citations in footnotes include dates of specific "sessions" of various "calls." Complete information is in Bibliography.]

SDT: Sovety deputatov trudiashchikhsia (Soviets of workers' deputies).

SGP: Sovetskoe gosudarstvo i pravo (Soviet state and law).

USSR Zasedaniia: Zasedaniia Verkhovnogo Soveta SSSR: stenograficheskii otchet. (Meetings of the USSR Supreme Soviet; stenographic report.) Moscow. [Citations in footnotes include dates of specific "sessions" of various "calls". Complete information is in the Bibliography.]

GLOSSARY OF RUSSIAN TERMS

APPARAT: the apparatus or professional bureaucracy; as most often used, it refers to the Party apparatus.

APPARATCHIK: one who works in the apparat.

GORKOM: literally, city committee (abbreviation of gorodskoi komitet). In this study it refers exclusively to the city Party committee, or Party gorkom.

GOSPLAN: the State Planning Commission. USSR Gosplan is centered in Moscow. Subordinate to it are republic branches—for example, Ukrainian Gosplan.

GOSSTROI: the State Construction Committee. USSR Gosstroi is attached to the USSR Council of Ministers. Branches include RSFSR Gosstroi.

ISPOLKOM: the executive committee (abbreviation of ispolnitel'nyi komitet). In this study the term refers exclusively to executive committee of a local soviet, as in city ispolkom.

NOMENKLATURA: the list of posts or jobs over which a particular Party organ has control; i.e., the right to nominate personnel or to approve hiring and firing.

RSFSR: the Russian Soviet Federated Socialist Republic, the largest of the fifteen Soviet republics.

TEB: the Technical-Economic Bases for a General Plan for the Development of Moscow until 1980.

ZAKAZCHIK: the body that finances a construction project, draws up plans, and concludes an agreement with a contractor (podriadchik).

Governing Soviet Cities

THE LESSONS
OF SOVIET CITIES

Soviet urban development is too important a subject to be left only to Soviet writers or to urbanists of East or West. Soviet city government is, I contend, a political process. Yet students of Soviet politics have neither appreciated that fact fully nor realized the extent to which the evidence of Soviet cities challenges conventional wisdom concerning the Soviet political system and the way it ought to be compared with the U.S. system.

CITY GOVERNMENT IS POLITICS

This book is based on the view that the day-to-day work-ings of city government . . . are best understood by look-ing at differences of interest and opinion that operate within cities, at issues which arise out of these differ-ences, and at the way institutions function to resolve (or fail to resolve) them. It is based, in short, upon a view of city government as a political process.[1]

These are the words with which Edward C. Banfield and James Q. Wilson began their 1963 study of city politics in the United States. They are words that aptly serve to introduce this book, too. Banfield and Wilson's was not the usual approach to their subject; nor has mine been to my subject, by either Soviet or Western standards.

American city government, wrote Banfield and Wilson, "is usually treated more as a matter of 'administration' than of 'politics'":

Those who write about it are, as a rule, more concerned with legal arrangements than with informal devices by

which things are actually done, more with the activities of
appointed officials (bureaucrats) than with those of elected
ones (politicians), and more with the procedures by which
routines are carried on than with the large forces that
determine the content of policy.

Banfield and Wilson "reverse the usual emphasis because we
think the nature of American government requires it":

> In many other countries it might be possible to identify
> some sphere—often a large one—that is almost purely
> "administrative" in the sense that matters are decided,
> as Max Weber said, according to rule and without regard
> to person. But in the United States there is no such sphere.
> Our government is permeated with politics. This is be-
> cause our constitutional structure and our traditions
> afford individuals manifold opportunities not only to bring
> their special interests to the attention of public officials
> but also—and this is the important thing—to compel offi-
> cials to bargain and make compromises. The nature of
> the governmental system gives private interests such
> good opportunities to participate in the making of public
> decisions that there is virtually no sphere of "adminis-
> tration" apart from politics.

Soviet city government has traditionally been viewed more as
administration than politics. Soviet writers describe "socialist
administration"—harmonious governance under the benevolent guidance
of the Communist Party. Most Soviet scholars devote little attention
to political conflict. They write as if all one needed to know were
legal norms and administrative rulings; they devote pages to constitutional theory, giving but few concrete examples, and conclude
that in most cases practice conforms to theory while in a few
unfortunate but surely temporary ones it does not.[2]
For a long time Western observers stood the official Soviet
description on its head. They viewed city government as an example
of totalitarian administration, a realm not of all-pervasive harmony
but of omnipresent centralization and Party manipulation. And
while Westerners emphasized informal controls, Soviet writers
stressed formal-legal authority; but neither group had much to say
about how things are actually done. Westerners focused on Party
apparatchiki behind the scenes, and Soviets focused on government
officials; but neither group dwelt on interrelationships among these
and others in city politics. Some Soviet scholars reported routine
administrative procedures, but linked these with a ritualized rendition

of the class forces that supposedly determine policy. For Westerners
who understood larger forces according to the "totalitarian model,"
the details of city government seemed of peripheral importance.

The "totalitarian model" of Soviet society depicted a monolithic
Party remolding an atomized society in accordance with established
ideology.[3] In recent years Western scholars have increasingly
questioned that picture, viewing it as insensitive to the presence of
politics and the reality of change. Hence while Soviet scholars have
taken to doing more empirical studies, Westerners have been re-
examining Soviet city government with an eye to flux and change as
well as centralization and uniformity. And yet the standard conception
of Party-dominated urban governance persists. In 1953 Merle Fainsod
quoted Stalin to the effect that local governments (soviets) were "a
transmission belt" linking Party and people, that they were "organizations which rally the laboring masses . . . under the leadership of the
Party." To which Fainsod himself added: "The soviets themselves
are Party-dominated. Responsibility for selection of membership
and for direction of their activities remains in the Party. In each
soviet the inner board of control is invariably a Party fraction."[4]
As late as 1972 an article entitled "Decision Making in Soviet Cities"
concluded that "The Communist Party stands squarely in the center
of this process making all the basic policies," and that while "the
nature and quality of this Party dominance may be changing, as
educational qualifications and professional expertise of urban Party
officials rise, these changes have not altered the basic fact of Party
dominance over decision-making."[5]

But saying that municipalities are Party-dominated does not
explain the dilemma of city officials who must cope with conflicting
instructions from higher Party bureaus. The inner board of control
in city administrations may be a Communist fraction, but equally
Communist are the factory managers and higher state officials whose
actions often confound city leaders. Finally, what is one to conclude
when vaunted centralized controls, far from ensuring monolithic
uniformity, instead become weapons for a local conflict in which
industrial interests have been as influential or even more influential
than urban Party officials?

In the face of such conflict, this book, like Banfield and Wilson's,
suggests another approach.[6] Soviet government like American government, is "permeated with politics"—not because constitutional structure and traditions offer individuals and groups the chance to compel
public officials to bargain and make compromises, but because public
officials can compel each other to do so; not because the governmental system gives private interests opportunities to participate
in the making of public decisions, but because the Soviet political
system is a huge bureaucratic arena in which bureaus compete,

bargain, and negotiate to such a degree that although all are officially
subordinate to one central leadership there is virtually no sphere
of administration immune from bureaucratic politics.

TECHNOCRATS VERSUS THE PARTY?

All of this bears on another standard conception concerning
the relationship between Party officials and "technocrats" in modern
and "post-modern" Soviet society. According to a number of Western
analysts, it is useful to view the USSR as a developing country now
undergoing the strains of a more advanced industrial condition, or
as "a mobilization system" seeking to navigate through a "post-
mobilization phase."[7] Stalin, it is said, used totalitarian means to
mobilize resources for a few overriding goals, primary among them
being industrial development. But eventually industrialization makes
for a more complex, more differentiated society, which requires
a more balanced kind of development. Samuel Huntington has called
this "the adaptive phase." In it, he says, the Party must deal with
"legal-rational challenges to its authority which are, in large part,
the product of its earlier successes." Chief among these is the
challenge from "innovative technocrats," for "innovators are not
the reds but the experts."[8]

There are, it should be pointed out, two schools of thought
concerning the red-expert relationship. The first sees the Party as
a powerful obstacle to progress. Drastic economic reforms, including
a devolution in the Party's guiding role, are said to be required to
boost economic growth and technological innovation in what Zbigniew
Brzezinski has called "the technetronic era."[9] Brzezinski, among
others, has made a case for political change, arguing that "the pro-
gressive transformation of the bureaucratic Communist dictatorship
into a more pluralistic and institutionalized system—even though still
a system of one-party rule—seems essential if its degeneration is
to be averted." In the long run, Brzezinski continues, "perhaps the
ultimate contribution to Soviet political and social development that
the CPSU can make is to adjust gracefully to the desirability, and
perhaps even the inevitability of its own gradual withering away."[10]

Technocrats versus the Party? Transformation or degeneration?
Not necessarily so, according to the second school. Increasingly
staffed by men and women with advanced technical education, the
Party apparat may perform the function of mediator and integrator
among rival bureaucratic agencies and conflicting social forces.[11]
Adds Huntington: "The conflict between the political generalist and
the managerial specialist is inherent but limited. A complex modern
society requires both increased functional autonomy for managerial

specialists and increased political authority for the central political leadership. Meeting this latter need is the principal function of the Party apparat. It is as essential to the system as the expert bureaucracy. . . . The innovators are not the reds but the experts. The Party apparatus, on the other hand, becomes a gyroscope instead of a motor."[12]

How does the evidence of Soviet cities illuminate this debate? It jibes with neither side's assumptions. The rule that "the innovators are not the reds but the experts" is surely too sweeping, but grant for the sake of argument that it holds true on many economic and technological issues. It is decidedly not the case, however, as far as urban and environmental reform are concerned. In these areas, industrial managers are not necessarily innovators, but they are often vigorous opponents of change that would erode positions of bureaucratic power constructed during the years of all-out industrialization. On urban and environmental issues the much-maligned Party apparatchik is indeed needed to rein in recalcitrant managerial specialists. Yet ironically the supposedly powerful Party secretaries are not powerful enough to dictate to influential industries whose activities adversely affect the pattern of urban development.[13]

PARALLEL PROBLEMS:
THE UNITED STATES AND THE SOVIET UNION

The preceding observation in turn challenges the notion that the Soviet system may be better suited than the American one for building and governing cities. This view takes off from a by-now-familiar diagnosis of America's urban illness. Of prime importance is what J. K. Galbraith has called "social imbalance"—the unequal relationship between "the supply of private goods and services and those of the state."[14] This imbalance has, Galbraith argues, both ideological and institutional roots: our traditional attachment to production— "central to our striving to reduce insecurity . . . to avoid or finesse the tensions anciently associated with inequality and its inconvenient remedies"; our conviction that what private enterprise produces is sacred while expansion of the public sector is not; our "industrial system," which operates to foster and pursue its primary goals ("the expansion of output, the increase in consumption, technological advance and the public images that sustain it") at the expense of other goals, including urban planning and environment reforms.[15]

On the political side there is said to be an excess of pluralism. Cities are governed by what a massive study of New York City called "a multiplicity of decision centers"—"party leaders, elected and appointed officials, the organized bureaucracies, numerous non-governmental associations, officials and agencies of other governments."[16] There is "a division of powers such that the real sources of the crisis of our time fall in a no-man's land among duly constituted but politically impoverished governments inside the metropolitan region."[17] Political conflict forces the city planner to abandon his role as technical adviser and become a mobilizer or political broker.[18] Prudent political brokers "temporize in the hope that disagreements will work themselves out, or that they (officials) will have time enough to inform themselves more fully about the situation, or that circumstances giving rise to clashes will pass and obviate the need for their action, or that one side or the other will lose heart and abandon its fight."[19]

Insufficient public planning and pluralism's drawbacks—those who stress both could be called "doubting liberals." Their conviction that something is drastically wrong, and their advocacy of more government planning, distinguishes them from conservatives—who don't think things are so bad and would hesitate to prescribe planning even if things were. The liberals' doubts about pluralism, which has so long been the linchpin of the liberal creed, divides them from radicals, who charge that concentrated corporate power combines with the ongoing momentum of industrial society to settle the most important questions without genuine pluralist competition.[20] Such liberal doubts are far from universal. But they are sufficiently intense to have inspired some to take the near-desperate step—for liberals—of invoking the Soviet example.

Edward Logue, master planner in New Haven, Boston, and New York State, is one who has praised Soviet progress: approximately 200,000 units of housing built in Moscow each year compared to something under 20,000 in New York City. (Mass production, one may add, enables the Soviets to produce for $3,000 to $3,500 a four-room apartment that would cost $10,000 in the United States.) While the USSR has developed what one U. S. official has called "the only technology in the world to produce acceptable low-cost housing on a large scale," the United States, says Edward Logue, "has seen no significant changes in the way housing is produced in the last sixty years."[21]

But more important than Soviet technical advantages are state ownership of land and a centralized political system. American urban development, says Logue, is "chaotic, incremental, unplanned, and undirected—at any level of government, most particularly at the suburban level." In the Soviet Union, "all these decisions are made publicly and after careful consideration from the top down." Logue has noted the existence of a chief city planner of the Soviet Union. "It is not clear," he says, "that we even have a chief planner in New York or anywhere else in the United States. And we certainly don't

have those other interesting functions: Chief Architect of the Soviet
Union, Chief Architect of Moscow, Chief Architect of Leningrad."

The USSR has a national urban settlement policy. The United
States needs one, Logue adds, to stem overpopulation of some areas
(the East, West, and Gulf coasts; and Great Lake shores), to revitalize less developed regions, and to encourage growth of middle-
sized cities. But Logue fears that "the extent of public authority
required" to make and implement such a policy is "nowhere on the
horizon," and that "we are not going to get it without some kind of
crisis that will be painful enough itself so that we would all prefer
to avoid it."

Ada Louise Huxtable, architecture critic of The New York Times,
has made a similar judgment. The Soviet city building program, she
reported on the 50th anniversary of the October Revolution, is "one
of the most interesting, if far from perfect chapters in the history
of man's struggle with his environment. In size, in scope, in boldness,
in spite of crudities, failures and sometimes ludicrous imperfections,
it is a singularly important undertaking of the twentieth century."22
Soviet sins of quality and style are grievous, in her opinion: "sterile
neo-classicism of straight endless avenues, vacuous squares, and
conventionally ruled off residential areas." But America's weak-
nesses are Soviet strengths. "The tragedy of Soviet building," she
wrote, "is the repetitive and uninspired nature of city and neighbor-
hood planning. The tragedy of the West is that it is impossible to
mobilize building codes, trade unions, resources and production for
the kind of coherent planning and problem solving that its sophisticated
talents could provide."23

Have the Soviets found the successful urban formula? This
book will answer "no," or at least "not yet." It will argue that, on
the contrary, the Soviet system has managed the twin feats of re-
producing the distortions of free enterprise under socialism and the
pitfalls of pluralism in a centralized state. Soviet urban development is also unbalanced, with industrial expansion and population
growth exceeding the supply of housing, and housing going up faster
than the expansion of municipal and consumers services. Soviet social
imbalance is also the product of an economic system that has attached
higher priority to production than to urban planning, and to a political
system that, contrary to its Western reputation, is "open" enough
to enable industrial managers to resist Party-sponsored change.
That is not to say, of course, that there are not basic differences
that should be clear from the start. While Moscow is probably the
Soviet Union's most successful city (Leningraders would no doubt
disagree), America's largest metropolis is among its most desperate.
Whereas the United States has a central city sickness (middle-and
upper-class suburbs are not, after all, so unpleasant), the edges and

outskirts of Soviet cities (strictly speaking there are no suburbs in
the U.S. sense) have difficulty obtaining essential services, including
running water and sewage facilities. The shops and consumer services
that most but not all Americans take for granted in the private sector
are included (or often not included) among municipal services in the
USSR. Each nation has, in short, a different mix of urban successes
and failures; their experiences reflect divergent paths of historical
development and contrasting political and economic systems. But it
is also true that the two systems have converged in a way that
neither's leaders wanted or anticipated—the failure to build and
govern satisfactory cities.

These are, in brief outline, the major arguments of this book.
They will be developed as follows: bureaucratic politics (Chapter 2);
historical overview (Chapter 3); formal-legal relationships (Chapters
4 through 6); and patterns of politics in cities of different size and
age (Chapters 7 through 10).

Before proceeding further, though, it is useful to present a brief
and inevitably schematic description of the overall governmental
framework in which city politics takes place. This has to include
some discussion of the city government (city soviet) proper, but it
must begin and end with the larger bureaucratic context, with the
variety of other agencies—Party as well as state, central as well as
local, industrial as well as municipal—that are important participants
in the political process that is Soviet urban governance.

THE BUREAUCRATIC FRAMEWORK

For those accustomed to less centralized states, this introduction to the Soviet governmental setup involves terms and relationships that take some getting used to. Yet the fact that the system
is centralized, with so many relationships formally spelled out,
makes it easier to present than the U.S. system would be. In fact,
given the nature of the beast we seek to describe, an organization
chart is not only possible but likely to be helpful. My diagram is, I
assure the chart-shy reader, a simplified synthesis and hence the
only one in the book for him or her to contend with.[24]

The chart depicts the structures of both the Communist Party
and the Soviet government. Note first the different levels of administration at which one finds government and Party organs. Let
us begin at the top and work down, concentrating for the moment on
the government side of the chart. At the highest level—the national
or all-union level—one finds organs responsible for the affairs of
the USSR as a whole; at the republic level are the Party and government organs of the Soviet Union's fifteen constituent republics.

Below the republic level is the provinces level. The provinces vary greatly in size; a province in the mammoth Russian Soviet Federated Socialist Republic (RSFSR), for example, may be as large as a European country or a U.S. state, whereas a province in one of the smaller Soviet republics may be no larger than a U.S. county. Equivalent to provinces, in the Soviet administrative scheme, are cities of republic subordination; that is, those cities with municipal administrations that are directly responsible (in ways discussed below) to republic government organs. Such cities—also referred to as republic-level cities—consist of the most important ones in each republic; for example, Moscow and Leningrad in the RSFSR, and Kiev and Sevastopol in the Ukraine.

Below the province level is the district or county level. This level includes cities of province subordination; that is, those cities (of 50,000 or more inhabitants in the RSFSR and Ukraine) reporting directly to province authorities. Below the district level is the city level. This category consists of cities (with a minimum population of 12,000 in the RSFSR) that have governments responsible to district or county agencies.

At each of the five levels of government, as the chart shows, there are a soviet (or legislature) plus executive agencies. At the all-union level there are the USSR Supreme Soviet with its Presidium, plus (to the right of them on the chart) the USSR Council of Ministers, which is theoretically responsible to the Soviet. Subordinate to the council are certain ministries and state committees, many of which play important roles in city affairs.

The ministries, it should be noted, come in two varieties at this level. All-union ministries operate directly (that is, without intermediate republic-level subordinates) those industrial enterprises that require "standardization of parts, united research and design efforts and close cooperation generally"[25] (including such enterprises as automobile industry, chemical and petroleum machine building, gas industry, transport construction, pulp and paper industry). Following the vertical line on the chart down from all-union ministries, we see their enterprises, which are labelled "non-city" to distinguish them from city-owned and operated factories and services. Non-city enterprises are (as discussed in later chapters) vitally important actors in city politics, because the success of municipal administration depends in large part on the ability of city leaders to influence those activities. And yet, as the chart clearly shows, city and non-city enterprises are separated by a bureaucratic gulf—each is part of a separate hierarchy, and the two hierarchies are linked only at the national level.

In contrast to the all-union ministries, the union-republic ministries operate at both the national and republic levels. Their

THE BUREAUCRATIC FRAMEWORK

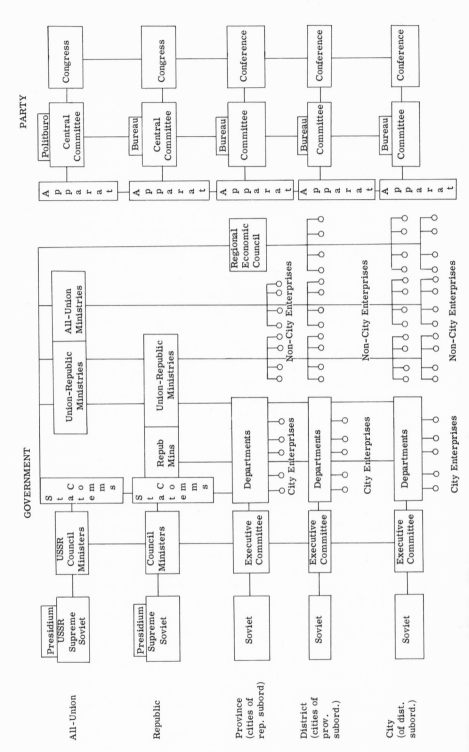

12

republic-level branches are "dually subordinate" both to the parent ministry in Moscow and to the council of ministers of the separate republics. Union-republic ministries are both industrial (chemical industry, food industry, light industry) and nonindustrial (finance, education, public health, trade). State committees, present at both all-union and union-republic levels, are responsible for coordination (or lack of same) among various ministries, and between cities and industrial agencies. Committees we shall be meeting again in the chapters that follow are the State Planning Commission (Gosplan), which assigns economic targets and resources to both city and non-city agencies, and the State Construction Committee (Gosstroi), subordinate to which is the Committee on Civil Construction and Architecture.

Of course each of the fifteen constituent republics has its own supreme soviet republic council of ministers. In addition there are republic ministries with no parent agency in Moscow that deal with matters thought not to require severe centralization. Of these, the ministries of housing and municipal services, guardian angels for municipal departments of the same name, play a leading role in our story.

At each level below the republic level the basic pattern is the same, and hence can represent the institutional structure of a typical Soviet city. This is, to be sure, an oversimplified picture, since government agencies differ in number, size, and subject matter in provinces, districts, and cities of different sizes. Nonetheless, the basic structure is the same in all.

In this book the municipal government will be referred to as the city soviet. Actually the term "soviet" has two uses. On the one hand it encompasses the city government as a whole; that is, the municipal organs seen along a horizontal line at each of the three urban levels. More narrowly, "soviet" refers to the city council, a large body of "elected" deputies whose powers, or rather lack of same, are described in Chapter 4. More important than the soviet in day-to-day administration is the municipal executive committee (ispolkom), which includes among its members local Party and industrial leaders, as well as heads of major municipal departments. In theory the executive committee is a kind of collective mayor; in fact the executive committee's chairman serves as mayor.

Subordinate to the executive committee (to its right on the chart) are municipal departments and administrations (e.g., planning; finance; architecture-planning; construction; education; municipal and consumers services; culture; trade; housing; general affairs). These operate city enterprises, which include not only the traditional municipal services familiar to Americans but also a variety of establishments (shops, consumers services, and local industries)

found in the private sector of a free enterprise system. The executive
committee as a whole and also most individual departments are (in
a manner described in Chapter 4) dually subordinate—that is, both
horizontally (the departments to the ispolkom, the ispolkom to the
soviet) and vertically (the departments to their superiors at the next
highest administrative level, the executive committee to theirs).

Next we turn to the Communist Party, on the right of the chart.
As described in Chapter 6, the Party has the formal mandate to
supervise governmental organs at all levels, and impressive resources
for carrying out this mandate. Furthermore Party and government
personnel interlock at all levels—from the top, where the prime
minister and other top state officials are members of the Party
Politburo or Central Committee, down to the cities, where the mayor
usually sits on the Party committee's bureau. At the urban level, the
Party apparat of full-time functionaries includes one or more Party
secretaries plus Party departments. The latter supervise the activities
of both municipal agencies and local non-city enterprises.

One final complication requires brief mention. The bureaucratic
framework depicted in the chart has not been constant, but rather
has been altered in important respects at various times by one or
another reform. Perhaps most important for a study of city politics
are the reforms of 1957 and 1965; the former abolished most industrial ministries and turned economic administration over to regional
economic councils, and the latter abolished the councils and reestab-
lished ministries. At first (following 1957) the councils paralleled
province boundaries—hence they are depicted at province level in the
chart. Later they were amalgamated and their superiors juggled in
a series of Krushchevian turnabouts too bewildering to follow, let
alone chart. The essential point is that between 1957 and 1965 the
councils acted as superiors to many non-city industrial enterprises
and hence became major participants in city politics.

2

CITY POLITICS AS
BUREAUCRATIC POLITICS

The purpose of this chapter is to present a bureaucratic politics approach applicable to Soviet city government. But first we must suggest why interest group analysis would be less useful.

Not so many years ago the idea of applying either approach to Soviet politics might have appeared fanciful. Totalitarian rule had been said to solve "the ancient dilemma of how to combine personal with public interest in such ways as to put an end to politics."[1] But increasingly, since Stalin's death and particularly in the aftermath of Khrushchev's demise, the totalitarian explanation has fallen out of favor. Did it not exaggerate the Party leadership's ability to control and direct society? Had not even Stalin's dreadful reach exceeded his grasp? Since Stalin's death the Soviet system had undergone major changes, including the abandonment of arbitrary terror. How could the totalitarian model explain the transformation?[2]

INTEREST GROUPS: EAST AND WEST

In recent years the field of Soviet studies has exploded with new approaches to Soviet politics, with attempts to combine (to quote the title of a recent collection) "the behavioral revolution and Communist studies."[3] Of these, one of the most popular has been the notion that the Soviet politics, like U.S. politics, revolves around the actions of political interest groups. Originally elaborated in the United States, group theory has taken two related but distinguishable directions in American political science. The more familiar approach—as developed, for example, in David B. Truman's The Governmental Process— deals with organized pressure groups (trade unions, farmers' groups, trade associations, etc), but extends its conceptual umbrella to cover

other phenomena as well—"potential groups" (unorganized interests),
"majority groups" (the electorate), "official groups" (bureaucrats and
governmental institutions). The other approach (actually the original
approach), which was founded in 1908 by Arthur Bentley, presents
groups less as real or reified entities and more as masses of human
activity moving in a common direction. The activity itself, or the
"tendencies of activity," is "the group."[4]

Both approaches have come under scholarly criticism in their
native land. The former, it has been said, reduces a wide variety of
social and political phenomena to one all-purpose and hence overworked
category. The latter is so amorphous that, as one critic has put it,
"It is difficult to see what 'group theory' means, let alone why anyone
should want to use it. . . ."[5] The debate goes on. Meanwhile a similar
debate, with reference to Soviet politics, begins.

Most group analysts of Soviet politics have adopted the more
structured American version. Brzezinski and Huntington have distinguished three sorts of groups: "amorphous social forces" (workers,
peasants, and others), "specific interest groups" (intellectual community, ethnic minorities), and "policy groups" (military, managers,
state bureaucrats).[6] H. Gordon Skilling has described two categories:
"occupational groups," including "intellectual groups" (writers,
economists, lawyers) and "official groups" (Party apparatchiki, state
bureaucrats, police); and "opinion groups" (liberal writers, centralist
economists, conservative military).[7] Yet neither these nor other
writers deny that most Soviet "groups" lack characteristics of the
Western species; that is, formal organization, autonomous resources,
consistent leadership, regular interaction among members, and finally
what Earl Latham has called "the indispensable ingredient of 'group-
ness'—consciousness of common interest, and active assistance,
mutually sustained to advance and promote this interest."[8] And most
group analysts are the first to state that Soviet pluralism is, as
Skilling puts it, at best only "incipient," since "the making of policy
remains highly centralized and authoritarian, with great power resting
in the hands of a few at the top, with groups playing only a secondary
role."[9]

Given these facts of Soviet political life, formulations to which
other Western writers have retreated seem as ghost-like as the
phenomena they are supposed to describe. For Philip H. Stewart,
"More than two people expressing publicly a similar opinion without
knowing of each other's existence is a grouping."[10] With several bows
to Arthur Bentley, Franklyn Griffiths describes not a clash of organized groups but rather a "system-dominant conflict of tendencies
of articulation through which specific values are allocated for society,"
a policy-making process "in which the interaction among individuals
who articulate policy expectations results in the emergence of, and

selection from, a series of alternate possible directions of value allocation—tendencies of articulation—for Soviet society."[11]

Neither interest group approach is as helpful as one would wish. Stewart's prejudges the issue by implying that Soviet groups will become more like their American counterparts. The amorphous conceptions—two-man groupings and tendencies of articulation—are not only logically and esthetically unattractive but cannot account for the powerful pressures and cross-pressures that have shaped the direction and pace of change in recent years. "The politics of communist parties," Andrew Janos has written, "is the politics of organizations and not of autonomous groups." This, Janos explains, is "not to say that Communist parties are immune from conflict and internal competition . . . but [that] the conflicts that arise are fought out or resolved in a hierarchical context, which gives politics a special quality."[12] That special quality, and its relation to change, are on display in Soviet cities.

GAMES SOVIET BUREAUCRATS PLAY

Bureaucracy has been a central theme for students and enemies of the USSR—two breeds that, Soviet allegations notwithstanding, are not necessarily synonymous. Trotsky described the "bureaucratic degeneration" of the Communist Party and Soviet state; so have revisionist critics in East Europe. Western studies have analyzed the structure of Soviet bureaucracies, their function in the political system, their leaders and elites. But we have not yet plumbed the full significance of the fact that the Soviet governmental system—in a sense a mammoth, complex organization—is riven up and down by bureaucratic politics; that Soviet policies and lack of policies, foreign as well as domestic, mirror the clashes and compromises, antagonisms and alliances, of powerful bureaucratic agencies and their representatives; that Soviet governmental behavior reflects not only the Politburo's deliberate political purpose—to the extent that that quarrelsome body has one—but also the mode of operation of complex large-scale organizations that even a powerful central leadership cannot always and everywhere control.[13]

Western experts have resisted the notion that studies of Western organizations can provide a guide to Soviet government. To Paul Hollander, for example, "the differences outweigh the similarities," for "the decisively distinctive feature" of Communist bureaucracies is "their thorough politicization, from which follow many other features setting them apart from Western bureaucracies."[14] But the politics of Soviet urban development is a species of bureaucratic politics whose primary features are well known in non-Soviet settings.

Let us consider six laws (like Parkinson's) of bureaucracy, culled from studies of Western organizations but applicable to Soviet city politics.[15]

The first law is that division of bureaucratic labor produces competition. Complex problems are sliced up and farmed out to organizational subunits. Each part of the problem remains just that for the organization as a whole, but not for its subunits. Bureaus lose sight of the big picture. They develop parochial perspectives from information gathered from their own sources and processed through their own channels. They pursue selfish interests—self-preservation and growth, as well as fulfillment of central assignments. They defend their territory. They resist encroachments—investigations by outsiders. They fear changes that would reduce the scope or importance of their functions, that would reduce resources needed to perform their duties, and that would increase responsibility without adding new resources.

The foundation of Soviet city politics is the division of bureaucratic labor. Local institutions—industrial, soviet, Party—have different stakes in urban development. Higher authorities have their own stakes as well. The result is competition within an overall hierarchical framework. The result of competition is that city planning is a political process in which many municipal planners can effectively influence neither the non-city sector nor, as is often the case, their own. Severe compartmentalization and extreme centralization accentuate competition; attached to separate subhierarchies, soviet and non-soviet agencies have a minimum of formal contact. Even when the two want to coordinate planning, the budget-plan drafting process makes it difficult for them to do so.

A second and related law is that organizations—like the individuals who constitute them—act incrementally. In the jargon of organization theory, bureaus engage in (1) "problem-directed search"—looking for an answer close at hand; (2) "satisficing"—accepting the first answer that looks good enough instead of insisting on the best; (3) "standard operating procedures"—routines that guarantee application of old answers to new problems. Incrementalism in Soviet cities involves industrial enterprises unwilling to take on more than their high priority production tasks, but equally unwilling, once they have built housing and services, to let them go; city governments unable to carry out their mandate, but also reluctant to seek greater responsibility; and, at the top, the central leadership taking initial steps toward urban reform in 1957, taking the next big step only in 1971.

Bureaucratic competition and incrementalism complicate planning and inhibit change. The third and fourth laws are that great size and scarcity, two conditions that characterize the Soviet governmental system, make coordination even more difficult. Gordon Tullock describes a phenomenon that has come to plague Soviet central planners—"bureaucratic free enterprise," a system that "more or less develops naturally when efforts are made to extend the size of an hierarchical organization beyond its practical limits." The larger the organization, "the smaller the percentage of its actions that represent directly the desires of the ultimate sovereigns of the organization, its higher officials."[16]

Scarcity at once increases the need for coordination and frustrates attempts to achieve it. Scarce resources must be rationed, but bureaus compete for them with particular intensity. Bureaucratic free enterprise is not likely to yield to coordinators who cannot or will not sweeten their exhortations with additional rubles.

The fifth law is that the center's efforts to counteract operation of the previous principles can make matters worse. A separate monitoring agency "imposes ever more complex and ever more restrictive regulations." A monitored bureau must "consume more and more of its resources to satisfy the demands of the monitors for information . . . and devote ever more resources to figuring out ways of evading or counteracting the monitor's additional regulations."[17]

In Soviet cities, as elsewhere in the Soviet system, the Party is the most important monitor. Yet the Party is itself divided. All the multiple antagonists in city politics—mayors managers upper level planners—are Party members. So much for Party membership alone as the basis for an interest group or even a tendency of articulation on the most important urban issues. The Party apparat is apparently more unified. Yet, to the extent one can follow their activities in the politically false-modest press, Party secretaries seem surprisingly ineffective, being unable to prevent disputes, and being unsuccessful in arbitrating them.

The sixth rule is as follows: when central leaders want to accomplish urgent tasks that require complex operations and considerable innovation, they must (1) "set up special organizations outside the normal bureaucracy"; or (2) launch special "campaigns" that focus attention and resources on high priority goals.[18]

During the years when the Soviet leadership took neither of these two steps—at least until 1971—city leaders tried variations of both.[19] While various municipal leaders fought or did not fight for reform within their own cities, a surprising number manifested enough group consciousness to campaign, in apparent coordination, for the common cause. In contrast to their American counterparts, Soviet officials formed no organized pressure group, no USSR Conference of Mayors. But they were more than a tendency of articulation. If the term "political group" or "political grouping" is to make sense in Soviet politics, it could be saved for cases like this—when leaders of different bureaus act in tandem, outside as well as through bureaucratic channels; when, like Soviet mayors, they lobby in newspapers and journals, and, for example, at Supreme Soviet sessions, which they seem to credit with more clout than do most Western observers. Soviet mayors may well view themselves in just this light. But they would also have to admit that they have not been as successful as managers who, without any visible intercity organization, and without any public counter-campaign, have worked through bureaucratic channels to resist change.

3

Moscow, June 1960. A national conference on soviet cities. In attendance—Politburo members including Brezhnev and Kosygin (but not the reigning Khrushchev), plus a thousand delegates from all across the USSR, among them mayors, planners, architects, economic administrators, and managers. The purpose of the conference: to evaluate forty-three years of Soviet urban development.[1]

The keynote speaker was V. Kucherenko, chairman of the USSR State Construction Committee (Gosstroi), highest official with direct responsibility for urban affairs. He discoursed first on the system's achievements and its fundamental soundness—self-congratulation so fulsome that one would have thought the USSR had become the promised Communist land. Next he listed "shortcomings"—an indictment so incriminating that one wonders how the oration's two parts could peacefully coexist.

To appreciate progress, said Kucherenko, one must look back to the pre-Revolutionary period, when Russian municipal services were "the most backward in Europe"; when 80 percent of urban housing was one or two stories high; when most homes were of wood, only one in ten had running water, and less than that were connected to sewage lines. Since the Revolution the nation's urban population had rocketed upward—from 18 percent of the total in 1926 to 49 percent in 1960. During the same period 700 new cities had been founded. In the midst of this urban boom, one may add, a prime planning goal had been balance—balance in the geographical distribution and size of cities (to avoid bloated megalopolis at one extreme and stagnant backwaters at the other), and balance in particular cities between industrial and population growth on one hand and the supply of housing and services on the other. What was to have made such a policy feasible was socialism—central planning and state

21

ownership of land. "Unfortunately," Kucherenko declared, "we still
make inadequate use of the basic advantages of socialist society."[2]

SHORTCOMINGS

The list of shortcomings (supplemented here by other Soviet
accounts from the same period) begins with what should have been
the strongest of strengths: regional planning—the coordination of
industrial and urban growth. The trouble with regional planning was
that not enough people were doing it, and those who were found themselves ignored. In 1952 a high Party official reported that the State
Planning Commission (Gosplan) "essentially confines itself to
industry-by-industry planning and has lost contact with the localities."[3] The pattern persisted. "You will not find regional plans on
the desk with truly important documents," observed B. Svetlichnyi,
a leading architect-official in 1966. "Instead, after a cursory examination, they are sent back to the people who drafted them."[4]

As for urban plans—theoretically a must for every city—they
were not to be found at all in a great many places in 1960. Of 1,700
Soviet cities, half had no plan. Of 875 in the RSFSR, 350 lacked plans,
as did 144 of 331 cities in the Ukraine and 48 of 64 cities in
Byelorussia. Among those lacking plans were Kiev, Sverdlovsk,
Novosibirsk, Gorky, Kharkov, and Odessa.

Cities with plans found them more or less useless. Such plans
were inaccurate, because Gosplan had not forecast economic prospects,
thereby leaving town planners without essential data; insensitive,
because the high level institutes that drafted them were too far away
to comprehend local problems; and out of date in the time needed to
prepare them (two and a half to three years for a city of 100,000 to
150,000). Not surprisingly city architects—functionaries with direct
responsibility for planning—were in short and shifting supply. Five
of twelve in the most important cities of Kazakhstan were not architects at all, but rather construction engineers. Six had come and
gone in rapid succession in both Gorky and Angarsk, as had five in
Novosibirsk. Only two educational institutions trained town planners,
and only 40 students matriculated in 1959.[5]

Soviet planners have argued about what constitutes optimum
city size, but the prevailing view—the Party line—has been that a
population between 50,000 and 200,000 is optimal, and anything more
than about 500,000 is undesirable.[6] Larger cities may offer economies
of industrial scale but at too high a cost in "reduced convenient space
for industry and housing, increased sanitation and health problems,
transportation tie-ups. . . ."[7] Undeveloped smaller towns need a
stimulating dose of industrialization; in return they offer abundant

labor (unemployment, the less generous may call it) and natural
resources. The Soviet leadership has tried to legislate balance. In
1931 the Party Central Committee declared it "inexpedient to create
giant cities with great numbers of enterprises," and banned most
new industrial construction in Moscow and Leningrad. In 1935
Moscow's urban plan limited the city's population to five million, and
in the same year the government prohibited construction of new
enterprises in Kiev, Kharkov, Rostov-on-Don, Gorky, and Sverdlovsk.
A passport system was devised to control immigration into heavily
populated centers.[8]

By 1960 the failure to achieve these goals was all to obvious.
In 1926 there had been only three cities with more than 500,000
inhabitants, the population of the three being 4.1 million, or 14.6
percent of the total urban population. By 1959 there were 25 such
cities, with 24.1 million people, or 23.9 percent of the urban total.[9]
Cities—Moscow and Leningrad in particular—in which expansion was
specifically discouraged by decree looked as if the law had encouraged
their growth (see Table 1). Across the nation, housing and city

TABLE 1

Population Growth of Seven Cities Following Approval of
Resolution to Prohibit Building of New Enterprises

City	Population (thousands) 1931 or 1939 (Year Prohibition was Announced)	1959	1970	Increase: 1970 over 1931 or 1935 Number (thousands)	Per- cent
Moscow	2,800 (1931)	5,086	7,061	4,261	252.18
Leningrad	2,228 (1931)	3,221	3,950	1,722	177.29
Kiev	847 (1939)	1,104	1,632	785	192.68
Kharkov	833 (1939)	934	1,223	390	146.82
Rostov-on-Don	510 (1939)	600	789	279	154.71
Gorky	644 (1939)	942	1,170	526	181.68
Sverdlovsk	423 (1939)	779	1,026	603	242.55

Sources: Narodnoe khoziaistvo v SSSR v 1964, pp. 22-31; "On
the preliminary results of the 1970 all-union population census,"
Pravda April 19, 1970, pp. 1-2; and Timothy Sosnovy, "Housing
Conditions and Urban Development in the U.S.S.R.," New Directions
in the Soviet Economy, Part II-B, Joint Economic Committee Subcommittee on Foreign Economic Policy, United States Congress, 89th
Congress, 2nd session (Washington, D.C., 1966), p. 537.

services were distinguished by their shortage, and by the haphazard
way they were mixed with industrial enterprises in poorly planned
neighborhoods and cities.[10]

Why the disappointments? Soviet writers, and Westerners as
well, have found answers in the economic and technological backwardness that the Soviets inherited, in the terrible destruction of war,
in the Communist Party's drive to industrialize.

AN HISTORICAL OVERVIEW

The cities of pre-Revolutionary Russia, like so many features
of Tsarist society, cried out for change.[11] Urbanization had been
lopsided. On the eve of World War I, one fifth of the total urban
population was concentrated in Moscow and St. Petersburg. Industries
had expanded with minimal if any regard for their workers' welfare
and the surrounding environment: factories had seized river banks;
freight depots and warehouses mushroomed along railroad tracks.
Housing near industrial plants was built "in great density and with
little consideration for light and air." Municipal governments were
"legally not entitled and financially not in a position to ameliorate
these conditions."[12]

The ideological baggage the Bolsheviks carried with them in
1917 contained urban hints both helpful and not so helpful.[13] Most
important was a commitment to planning and a determination to
govern—two attitudes that now seem rather ordinary until one realizes
that the American tradition, for one, has included neither. Furthermore, since city planning as it is known today is largely a product
of the twentieth century, the Soviets could proceed unencumbered by
a detailed mid-nineteenth-century blueprint sanctified because Marx
and Engels had penned it. On the other hand the founders did provide
a general mandate (in The Communist Manifesto) gradually to abolish
the distinction between town and country, a piece of advice that implied
that cities must be kept smaller than in fact they could be (see the
Soviets' failure to limit big city growth) and that the countryside may
be built up more than perhaps it should be (witness one Nikita
Sergeevich Khrushchev's ill-fated agro-cities). As leader of a self-
designated proletarian revolution, Lenin could not fail to appreciate
the importance of cities, but once in power he was more concerned
with economic planning than town planning. Industrialization, counted
on by the Bolsheviks as the way to build Marxian socialism in backward Russia, would propel urban development along at a furious
pace—too furious, as Soviet city planners implied in the late 1950s,
when they reassessed the road they had travelled.

World war, revolution, and civil war did nothing to improve the condition of Russian cities. In the beginning the regime concentrated on restoration of industrial enterprises and on new housing— experimental, communal apartments for the new revolutionary age, and private homes as concessions to the previous age. "Recreational and cultural amenities received scant attention," one Western observer reports, "and no standards and norms were available for educational, sanitary and other services." Later there were new suburbs, new settlements, and new industrial towns. But new cities lacked effective plans, and "in existing cities plans did not extend beyond the introduction of zoning."[14]

With the 1930s came five-year national economic planning, and with it the basis, in theory at least, for regional and city planning on a broad scale. But the drive to industrialize established a different pattern. Production came first. Housing and city services were accorded lower priority.* Factories had more than their share of the country's resources. City soviets and city planners had less. "We all remember those not so distant years," Svetlichnyi recalled in 1966, "when ministries and factories literally tore cities apart, each trying, by fair means or foul, to build 'its' houses hard by the factory gates, to create, at any cost, 'its' residential district with 'its' water supply, 'its' sewage system, 'its' heating plant, club, small store—in a word everything for itself and nothing for the city."[15]

In a time of scarcity, industries sought self-sufficiency—except that, given an opportunity, they tried to stint on their own housing and services as well. The culprit was overambitious planning, which established targets demanding more than factories had the capacity to produce. In view of that pressure, managers had to maximize "productive" investment. Spending on housing and services was not productive: better living conditions might boost labor efficiency, but where labor was in adequate supply and the key criterion of success was output, not profits, low labor productivity was unfortunate but not critical.[16] How then to minimize "unproductive" investment? Answer: build in large cities where soviet-operated services already existed. Industrial construction might demand increased city

---

*Sosnovy reports ("The Soviet City," pps. 327-29) the following: (1) that investment in public housing construction dropped from a total of 22 percent of total investment in the national economy between 1918 and 1928 to 11.7 percent during the first five-year plan (1929-32) and 10.2 percent during the second plan (1933-37); and (2) that actual housing construction amounted to only 55.4 percent and 41.9 percent of planned goals during the first two five-year plan periods.

spending, but factories did not have to take that cost into account.
They were interested in what a worker produced, not what a city
spent on him. "There is nothing mysterious about it," wrote
Svetlichnyi:

> It is simply that day-to-day economic considerations
> often supersede theoretical principles. Today it is
> almost always cheaper to build new plants in a large
> city with developed industry and adequate transportation
> facilities, electricity and water, than in a remote
> town where as yet there is nothing, where everything has
> to be built almost from scratch . . . even though this is
> anything but sound for the greater economy of tomorrow.
> This is why people keep streaming into the cities and why
> all local measures—limitations on registrations, establish-
> ment of "rigid city limits" and "barriers" of woods and
> parks—prove useless.[17]

Meanwhile, war came again. The results were shattering:
1710 cities and towns destroyed; Stalingrad, Minsk, and Sevastopol
in utter ruins; Kiev, Kharkov, Rostov-on-Don gravely damaged;
70,000 villages, 6,000,000 buildings, and 37,000 industrial enterprises
demolished; 20 million people dead; 25 million people homeless.[18]
      And after World War II came reconstruction, with civilians and
military personnel clearing the rubble, and construction workers
housed in primitive barracks. Vital facilities were rebuilt first and
with great haste; again, as rebuilding continued, priority was given
to production.
      Against this background how can one judge the Soviet urban
record uncharitably? Soviet writers do not. Achievements, they say,
outweigh shortcomings. Most problems are the unfortunate by-
product of an industrialization process that was vital for national
defense and the future of socialism. In any case, they say, the USSR
has since begun to solve its urban problems. Since 1957 the leadership has recognized and dealt with them, so that (given the system's
fundamental soundness) improvement is only a matter of time.
      Many Soviets could probably agree with Robert Osborn's
description of "a mixture of successes and failures" and with his
conclusion, in 1969, that there is "no reason to judge the failures
harshly."[19] As Osborn notes,

> Until the 1950's there was hardly any remedy for these
> shortcomings in view of national investment priorities.
> New industries in new locations had to assure themselves
> of at least minimal housing and services in order to retain

a labor force at all. If they had waited for urban planners and municipal administrators to settle on integrated development plans, then waited still more until permanent apartments, utilities and all the rest were assured, one can well imagine the fate of production targets in the early five-year plans.

High priority industries not only got priorities in funds and material resources, but the best technical and managerial talent as well. While all this did grievous damage to urban planning of the future in view of the planning mistakes that were made, it could hardly have been otherwise. To this extent the Soviet Union's experience followed that of other industrial nations which experienced periods of rapid industrial growth.[20]

It is possible for one to find support for this view in American economist Albert O. Hirschman's contention that unbalanced growth produces the possibility of balanced growth? Hirschman defines balance as a rough equilibrium between the increase in social overhead capital (SOC), including municipal services, for example, and directly productive investment (DPA)—industrial and agricultural. An excess of SOC is the wrong kind of imbalance since it invites but does not compel a corresponding surge of DPA. On the other hand an "SOC shortage that is experienced as such is bound to lead to attempts to remedy it on the part of those who suffer from it or stand to gain from its elimination."[21]

Hirschman cites the USSR, along with Turkey and Japan, as countries that have experienced the better sort of shortage. Urbanization is a case in point:

Rapidly growing centers will usually suffer shortages, sometimes because of lack of proper planning, but often also because it would be illegitimate and wasteful to expand SOC facilities in anticipation of the kind of extremely rapid economic progress that does hit a city or areas sometimes, but whose occurence or continuation can never be predicted with confidence. When these shortages do occur, they do not seem to affect the growth perceptibly, but rather are taken as an additional proof that dynamic development is indeed underway. In an underdeveloped country it is often the city with the worst water, power and housing shortages that is most favored by private investors.[22]

One could ask Osborn why the priorities that did grievous damage to urban planning (and to many other things and people as well) could not have been otherwise. One wonders whether Hirschman condones the particularly severe imbalance in Soviet urban growth. Equally important, however, is that such analyses—especially the Soviets'—neglect politics; they neglect the way the political system has functioned not only to implement the old industry-first-cities-be-damned priorities but also to aggravate their impact on urban development and to inhibit efforts to change. What happens when "those who suffer or stand to gain" attempt remedies? They find that old evils have a powerful inertia, that institutional arrangements devised to implement one set of priorities resist efforts to set new goals, that bureaucratic interests that gain from an old order fight to perpetuate their position, that even a powerful central leadership may find it difficult to overcome these obstacles, especially when the leaders cannot bring themselves to break fully with the assumptions of an earlier era, of which they themselves are a product.

REFORMS AND AFTER

When Kucherenko addressed the national urban conference in 1960, reforms had been underway for at least three years. The changes took various forms, but perhaps the main thrust was this: city soviets were to be given more responsibility for ensuring balanced urban growth, and more resources to carry out their mandate. Industries were to surrender certain properties and prerogatives to the city governments, and to cooperate with soviets in advancing the general urban welfare.

In July 1957 the Party and government decreed that, beginning in 1958, each city soviet would act as zakazchiki for "all construction of housing, and municipal, consumer and cultural services carried out contractually."[23] As zakazchik (the verb "zakazat'" means "to order," and zakazchik is usually translated as "customer" or "client") the city would finance projects, draw up plans, and conclude agreements with contractors. Until 1957 non-city agencies and enterprises had been their own zakazchiki, in which capacity many had resisted soviet efforts to set standards for and coordinate their projects. The importance of a city being its own zakazchik was that city officials would thereby have direct control over housing and service construction.

Later the same year (1957) the central government turned its attention to existing housing and services. City dependence on enterprise-operated facilities had reduced the city soviets' capacity to deal forcefully with the owners. In December 1957, the central

government instructed the republic governments to arrange transfer
of these properties to local soviet jurisdiction.[24] Meanwhile city
governments were also to receive certain "local" industries transferred from ministerial control—industries described by one Soviet
writer as "small and technologically unsophisticated, but using
abundant local raw materials, employing otherwise unoccupied hands,
and supplying local populations with goods which God knows are not
very complicated but which the population knows are necessary."[25]

Implicit in these changes, or so city leaders thought, was the
promise of increased resources (funds, men, materials)—some to be
transferred from enterprises along with nonindustrial properties,
some in the form of greater central subsidies. Explicit was yet
another pledge to halt urban sprawl. "It is necessary at long last,"
said Khrushchev in 1958, "to put an end to population growth in big
cities through the influx of people from other areas of the country."[26]
In December of that year, Gosstroi issued specific guidelines: cities
with more than 250,000 inhabitants were off-limits for most new
industrial construction; industries were encouraged to expand in
cities of less than 100,000 and particularly in those of less than
50,000.[27]

Who initiated the process of change? It seems clear that "those
who suffered" did not: there were no pressure groups of concerned
citizens, little or no public lobbying by city officials before 1957.
The central leadership itself precipitated the change, a fact which
fits the standard conception of how the Soviet system operates.[28]
But what happened after 1957 does not fit. Implementation was uneven, erratic, and incomplete; subsequently many city leaders did
begin to exert pressure.

The central government's instructions had been ambiguous.
Balanced urban development should have higher priority, but industrial
production was still uppermost. "All Party and state organs" were
called upon to "extend the rights of local soviets,"—a slogan that
became the rallying cry of city leaders pressing for change. But the
same 1957 Central Committee resolution complained that soviets
were not using rights already granted to them by the constitution,
an accusation later to be cited by those who resisted the 1957
reforms.[29] The leadership apparently did not consider the situation
so urgent that it was willing to focus its attention and commit scarce
resources in an all-out campaign. By and large it left implementation
to subordinate agencies, expecting them to tailor programs to local
circumstances. But absence of a campaign gave free rein to a
political struggle in which the soviets were at a disadvantage, in

which bureaucratic inertia, even in city government ranks, ran counter
to the reforms themselves.*

The new era proceeded with what black Americans would
recognize as "all deliberate speed." The 1958 national economic
plan made no provision for transfer of zakazchik authority, and the
1959 blueprint did so only partially.[30] What should have been the

----

*Establishing the presence or absence of a central campaign
requires a subjective judgment. The 1960 Conference on Urban
Development was a sign of high-level interest, as were the numerous
newspaper articles on which Chapters 7 through 10 of this book are
largely based. On the other hand, top Party leaders have been con-
spicuously reticent—compared, for example, with their closer attention to implementation of the 1965 economic reforms—about the
political tug-of-war between city soviets and industrial enterprises.
The 1961 Party program promised that "the rights of local soviets
will be extended" so that they "will make the final decision on all
questions of local significance" [Programme of the Communist Party
of the Soviet Union (Moscow: Foreign Languages Publishing House,
1961), p. 86]. But First Secretaries Khrushchev and Leonid Brezhnev
have discussed urban issues in terms either so general or so technical
that they seem almost unaware of controversy. (See Khrushchev's
report to the Central Committee in Plenum CC (November 19-23),
pp. 40-41; and Brezhnev's to the Twenty-third Party Congress in
Pravda (March 30, 1966), p. 3. Nikolai Podgorny, chairman of the
highest soviet of all (the USSR Supreme Soviet), spoke thus at the
Twenty-third Congress:

. . . they [soviets] must be strict with all economic organizations, regardless of subordination, located on their territory; they
must suppress the selfishness of vested interests. Unfortunately
such selfishness occurs all too often—departmental blinders prevent
some managers and bureaucrats from using all their resources to
improve service to the population, to improve construction of housing,
childrens' institutions and municipal services. This is exactly where
the local soviet and its Executive Committee should show their
initiative and persistence.

In recent years, on the initiative of the Central Committee, the
powers of local soviets have been expanded. However, further increase is necessary and requires giving them greater independence
in deciding economic, financial, land and other questions.

This necessity determines the Party's course—to transfer to
local soviets, the power to decide once and for all, all local issues.
At the same time, though, soviets must use in full measure those

city soviets' right by law became the object of a political conflict.
Various soviets obtained different versions of the new authority.
Some complained that they could not use it effectively due to interference from higher agencies and overly complicated bureaucratic
procedures. All learned that construction financed with enterprise
incentive funds[31] was not covered by the reform, a fact that became
particularly important when those funds were increased and cities'
access to them reduced by economic reforms (in 1965) designed to
boost production.*

Transfer of existing housing and services went even more
slowly. Republic governments took their time. Municipalities did
manage to obtain delivery in certain cities; these cities are so
regularly referred to in Soviet sources merely as "Moscow, Leningrad,
and many other cities in the RSFSR and other republics," that one
begins to suspect that either the Soviet writers do not know what
those other cities are or that they are keeping their identity secret
for reasons of state security.[32] In 1963 the Ukrainian Supreme
Soviet was just "posing the question" of transferring enterprise
housing, and the others seem to have moved no faster.[33]

Most erratic of all was the transfer of local industries—so much
so that those local soviets that had received them promptly lost them
again to the regional economic councils. Neither the giving nor the
taking away followed a uniform pattern. "Republic governments
responded to separate requests from Party and soviet organs in
different regions, provinces and autonomous republics—with the
result that the number and type of enterprises subordinate to local
soviets of the same level and in the same areas were often quite
different."**

---

rights granted to them by the Constitution. Such rights have not been
used by them to anywhere near the extent necessary. The level of
organizational work of soviets is still too low. They still do not show
enough initiative. See Pravda, April 1, 1966, p. 4.

*The two central features of the 1965 reforms were (1)
abolition of regional economic councils and reestablishment of
industrial ministries, and (2) a reduction in central instructions for
economic enterprises.

**Chkhikvadze, Pavlov, and Azovkin, "Increasing the Role of the
Soviets," p. 15. The argument for taking local enterprises away
again was that regional economic councils were better equipped to
manage them. But many such enterprises brought their new managers
more troubles than profits and so were shut down—with the result
that localities had to buy at a great distance and pay a great deal to
transport, those goods which they had produced at lower cost at home.

Statistics on central contributions to municipal budgets are not generally available to foreign analysts. It would seem (see Chapter 4) that subsidies did rise substantially after 1958, as did overall state investment in housing and city services. But the increases were not enough to satisfy city leaders.

Statistics on urban population are available. They show that the latest effort to regulate growth has largely failed. Between 1959 and 1970 the number of cities with more than 500,000 inhabitants rose from 25 to 33, and their combined population rose from 24.2 to 37.2 million, or 27.4 percent of the urban total. During the same years seven more cities joined Moscow and Leningrad in the one-million-plus club, and approximately eleven more swept to within striking distance of that goal.*

Finally, in March 1971, the Party and government issued another round of urban resolutions and decrees covering the same questions addressed in 1957. The Central Committee's March 14 resolution was entitled, without trace of a smile, "On measures to further improve the work of city soviets" [emphasis added]. A week later the USSR Supreme Soviet's Presidium set forth "The basic rights and duties of city soviets," and the USSR Council of Ministers offered "Measures for strengthening the material and financial base of city soviet executive committees."[35]

The indictment was familiar. City soviets, said the Central Committee, are "still not making full use of their rights and possibilities to improve services to the population." Their most

---

The 1965 reforms apparently reversed course yet another time, transferring an unspecified number of enterprises back to local jurisdiction again. For more details see David Cattell, "Local Government and the Sovnarkhoz in the USSR, 1957-1962," Soviet Studies, XV, 4 (April 1964), pp. 430-42.

*Jerry Hough concludes, on the basis of statistical analysis, that the political leadership showed an increased ability to shape the pattern of urban population growth between 1959 and 1970. The relationship between city size in 1959 and rate of growth between 1959 and 1970 was "curvilinear: 1,000,000+ —21 percent; 500,000-999,999— 34 percent; 300,000-499,999—39 percent; 200,000-299,999—43 percent; 150,000-199,999—50 percent; 125,000-149,000—39 percent; 100,000-124,999—35 percent." Hough also recognizes, however, that "the percentage of the total population in cities over 500,000 in the country grew more rapidly, for 9 entire cities moved into this category for the first time in the census period." See Hough, "Soviet Urban Politics and Comparative Urban Theory," Comparative Public Administration, (November 1972).[34]

unfortunate shortcoming was their failure to promote "integrated
urban development" by "coordinating the work of enterprises and
organizations of different departmental subordination. . . ." But the
fault was not entirely or even mainly the cities', for while "the
constant numerical growth of urban population makes ever higher
demands on housing and municipal services . . . in many cities, the
soviets have no direct relationship to the maintenance, repair and
improvement of public housing, almost two thirds of which belongs
to non-soviet enterprises, institutions and organizations." Too many
city governments were "tolerating" enterprise under-fulfillment of
housing and service construction plans; other soviet leaders were
guilty of the contrary sin—illegally "binding" factories to "bear
gratuitous expenditures for local needs." But city Party authorities,
instead of gently guiding city governments, either still engaged in
"petty tutelage" or ignored the executive committee in order to deal
directly and apparently in alliance with economic managers.

The 1971 program of action mixed old and new recipes. The
Party's general injunction to soviets was, as before, "to work out
and implement in each district and city a complex of concrete
measures" aimed at improving housing and services, and "to step up
efforts to coordinate the work of all enterprises, institutions and
organizations located on their territory." A main element of reform
was "further transfer" to municipal control of non-soviet facilities,
and "wider introduction of the practice of city soviets acting as
zakazchik for housing and service construction." What was new in
1971 was somewhat greater specificity about what sorts of facilities
should be transferred to city soviets, when they should be turned
over, and what new resources and powers the cities' governments
would require to carry out enlarged responsibilities.

"Enterprises, institutions and organizations that primarily
serve the city's population" should be under city soviet control.[36]
"Appropriate state agencies" (apparently led by republic councils of
ministers) were to "establish procedures and deadlines for the gradual
transfer to the local soviets of enterprise housing and services, with
the simultaneous strengthening of the soviets' material, and construction and repair base" [emphasis added].[37] To facilitate such
"strengthening," (1) non-soviet organizations (with the exception of
all-union enterprises) would be required to turn over a percentage
of their profits to the cities in amounts and according to procedures
still to be defined; (2) republic governments were instructed to
"consider and resolve upon" additional steps to augment municipal
income; and (3) city soviets were given "the right to establish, with
the agreement of enterprises, joint utilization of funds earmarked

for housing and services.'* The new Supreme Soviet decree, a model
statute designed to set a pattern for republic decrees to follow,
responded to another longstanding request by setting down in one
authoritative place all the major rights and responsibilities of city
governments. Republic governments were given the task of making
certain that all other statutes affecting urban governance were in
accord with the basic USSR decree.

Such a barrage of legislation and instructions, launched by the
nation's most important political institutions, was impressive indeed.
Yet read in the light of the 1957 decrees and the intervening years,
the new laws offer some cause for skepticism. After fourteen years,
the central leadership appeared to have provided just what had been
lacking—massive, high-level intervention designed to speed the pace
of change. But a close look reveals signs of further compromise
and possibilities for further delays. After fourteen years the leadership was still urging only "gradual" change, was still leaving key
questions of procedures and timing to be defined at lower levels,
was still raising questions to be "considered" and at some unspecified
time to be "resolved."

Will the 1971 decrees prove more effectual than those of 1957?
Or will the same forces that made a second round of resolutions
necessary ensure for them a fate similar to that which befell the
first? How many of those forces—how many of the many problems
that this overview of Soviet urban development have revealed—are
generated by the basic bureaucratic framework, codified but not
substantially altered by the 1971 Supreme Soviet decree? (For a
schematic depiction of the basic bureaucratic framework, see the
chart in Chapter 1.)

---

*Additions to municipal budgets included some that seem so
natural that one would have thought they would have been granted to
city soviets long ago—for example, "leaving at the disposal of the
district and city soviets executive committees": (1) "the revenues
obtained additionally during execution of the budget . . . and through
the overfulfillment of revenues or through savings in expenditures";
and (2) "part of the profits of their subordinate enterprises providing
services to the city. . . ." For more on sources of municipal revenue
see Chapter 4.

4

INSIDE THE CITY SOVIET

According to law, city soviets govern Soviet cities. But who runs the city soviets? One can attempt an answer in general terms because the law stipulates a basic governmental structure for all cities, with fairly uniform variations in cities of different size.

SOVIET AND EXECUTIVE COMMITTEE

Soviet city government consist of two branches—a soviet (council) of deputies and an executive committee (ispolkom), which directs the municipal bureaucracy. Soviets in session are large congregations of unsalaried "elected" deputies (as many as a thousand in Moscow) who meet no more than six times a year. Executive committees (up to about twenty-five members) include key municipal department heads, as well as representatives of the city Party committee and important non-city agencies. The chairman, vice-chairman and secretary are full-time, paid city executives, with the chairman acting in effect as mayor.[1]

How do the branches divide responsibility? Is the soviet session a legislative activity and the ispolkom an executive branch in the Western sense of those terms? Soviet writers say no; they say soviets are unique institutions that intertwine executive and legislative functions—all executive committee members being deputies and all deputies able to take part in supervising the administration.[2]

According to law the soviet session is preeminent. It alone has the authority to decide the most crucial questions; that is, to approve the city budget, to adopt plans for the city-run enterprises, to issue ordinances, and to elect the executive committee, hear its reports, and approve its nominations for heads of departments.[3]

In theory, executive committees govern in the interim between soviet sessions; they implement the law, direct departments that operate municipal enterprises, guide executive committees of soviets subordinate to the city soviet, (the nature of such relationships is described below), receive complaints from citizens, and allocate city land to non-city agencies. In fact, however, executive committees dominate their soviets.

There is no question that this was the case under Stalin, when flagrant abuses were the rule: "Deputies were not accountable before their electorate; executive committees took over the work of soviets; sessions were called irregularly in violation of the law; and questions of interest to the workers were hardly ever placed on the agendas of meetings which were held."[4]

Since Stalin's time, mayors have used more subtle means, ones familiar to observers of governments outside the USSR. The executive committee convenes the soviet session, sets its agenda, drafts legislation for it to consider, and prepares material for it to discuss— with the result, Soviet scholars say, that sessions do not manifest much independence.[5] The budget-drafting process is scheduled so that when the session sees "its" budget, time remains for only minor changes. But deputies rarely object. Seldom do they employ their constitutional power to call departments "to account"; almost never do they "recall" recalcitrant city leaders. Even the session's right to hire and fire its staff is hollow; executive committee members formally elected by the session are in reality chosen by Party and higher soviet bureaus.[6]

During the early 1960s much was made in the Soviet press of deputy and volunteer groups that were supposed to monitor and, in some cases, take over duties of municipal departments. Soviet standing committees, for example, are responsible only to the soviet session;[7] in reality, though, they depend on the administrators they are supposed to supervise. The organization-instruction department provides standing committees with office space, technical assistance, and information. Deputies probe and goad and persuade, but when persuasion fails, most of them find their only recourse is the executive committee. The same dilemma confronts deputies' groups, individual deputies, volunteer councils attached to city departments, and street and house committees charged with improving neighborhoods.

"At the present time," wrote the chairman of the State Law Department of Leningrad University in 1967, "standing committees and deputies' groups work not only with the assistance of the executive committees, which is, of course, necessary, but in fact under their very direction, which diminishes their ability to control the ispolkom."[8] Moscow University researcher V. Razin put it more succinctly: executive committee cadres "treat deputies the way Young Pioneer counselors treat the Young Pioneers."[9]

Then there is the voter. He has only one Party-approved candidate to choose from in the voting booth, but can make use of an "instruction" to inform the city government of his wishes. According to the authoritative Bulletin of the executive committee of the Moscow city soviet, an instruction adopted by voters meeting during election campaigns is binding on the soviet. But voters, like deputies, may expect guidance. "It is very important," counsels the bulletin, "that competent representatives of the executive committee and of Party and other public organizations take part in the discussion. These people are well enough informed so that they can help explain which suggestions are worth formulating as instructions and why some would be impossible to fulfill. . . ."*

THE CITY AND ITS SUPERIORS

"Dual subordination": This is the ingenious administrative principle according to which (1) the executive committee is subordinate to its counterpart at the next highest level of government, as well as to its city soviet; and (2) municipal departments report not only to their executive committee but also to higher-level departments, or to ministries for which departments at various levels are in effect constituent bureaus.**

Dual subordination is designed to blend central coordination with local initiative. If no outsider can precisely gauge the balance of central and local authority, Soviet writers cannot either. One expert writes that "dual subordination does not constitute a balance between horizontal and vertical power," that "horizontal lines emerge more clearly and distinctly."[11] But there is ample evidence of predominant central power.

Armenian Supreme Soviet chairman I. Arutunian has reported that "of all the decrees which in one way or another define the authority

---

*Once adopted, an instruction should be forwarded to the new soviet in session. Only the soviet may decide which instructions can be carried out, and which, because they do not conform to the years plan, cannot. But such a decision can only be made on the basis of information supplied by the executive committee, and once the decision is taken, the executive committee carries it out. In practice, many instructions are adopted or rejected in the ispolkom and never reach the soviet session at all.[10]

**For a schematic depiction see the chart in chapter 1. Whether city officials report to district, province, or republic authorities depends on their city's "level or subordination."

of local soviets, more than half are instructions of all-union agencies."
He called these the "swollen cheeks" of central power. Centralization
in the field of finance may be natural, he wrote, but surely the USSR
ministries of health and of culture need not dictate all but the smallest
operational details for local departments and volunteers' councils
which aid them.[12] The Academy of Sciences' Institute of State and
Law has deplored the ministries' habit of controlling local departments "by the back door."[13] And local officials continually urge
ministries to offer only technical aid, leaving operations, including
recruitment and training of personnel, to local authorities.[14]

David Cattell found four kinds of municipal departments in
Leningrad: (1) those that were in effect branches of higher agencies
and hence received directives, resources, and department heads
from above (finance, architecture-planning, construction, construction
materials, education); (2) those that, though attached to ministries,
also answered to an executive committee that "appears to have some
discretion in the nomination of the chiefs of these departments"
(social security, general food supplies, municipal and consumer
services, culture, trade, local industries, and others); (3) those over
which central authorities "exercise only general supervision" (gas,
roads and bridges, water and sewage, housing, housing allocation,
capital repairs, movie theaters, parks and gardens, tram-trolleybus,
water transport, and subway management); and (4) service departments of the executive committee (general affairs, organization-
instruction, cadres, etc.).*

Municipal budgets reveal city soviet dependence.

The city's own independent sources of income include the
following:

1. Deductions from profits of municipal enterprises, including
services and municipally operated industries.

2. Local taxes, including those on building and rents, autos
and other means of transportation, and collective farm markets.

---

*Cattell, Leningrad: A Case Study of Soviet Urban Government,
pp. 48-50. Some municipal bureaus are called administrations rather
than departments, a distinction that, being none too clear in Soviet
sources, is not observed here. Smaller cities have fewer departments,
a fact noted with examples by Gabrichidze, Gorodskie sovety, pp.
192-98. As an example of dual subordination, one can cite departments
of architecture and planning (sometimes called "construction and
architecture"). These report to province agencies, which in turn
report to republic branches of the State Committee on Construction
and Architecture, which is itself subordinate to the USSR State
Committee on Construction.

3. Income tax on cooperatives and public organizations (trade unions, sports societies, clubs, etc.).

4. State duties on legal administrative services (notary public, etc.).

Higher authorities supply a major proportion of urban revenues. Revenue sent down from on high is called "regulated income." It consists of (1) deductions from turnover tax levied on state enterprises and economic organizations; (2) personal income tax; and (3) tax on bachelors and small-sized families.[15]

Table 2 shows city soviet revenues at various times between 1946 and 1962. The rise in total income is substantial, particularly after 1955; but most of the increase came from central sources, while the percentage of independent income has declined.* One reason for the decline was the abolition in June 1959 of the tax on buildings and rents of state enterprises and public organizations, a change that

TABLE 2

City Soviet Revenues from Local Sources, 1946-62

Year	Total Income of all City Soviets in USSR (billions of rubles)*	Income from Local Sources Amount (billions of rubles)*	Percent of total
1946	1,700.3	1,101.0	64.8
1950	2,558.4	1,347.6	52.7
1955	5,332.2	2,959.9	55.5
1960	7,683.9	3,096.4	40.3
1962	8,731.8	3,233.1	37.1

*One ruble is officially valued at $1.11. All figures in this book are given in terms of this value.

Source: N. Shirkevich, Mestnye biudzhety SSSR (USSR local budgets) Moscow: Finansy, 1965), p. 52.

---

*Shirkevich reports (Mestnye biudzhety, p. 59) that cities most dependent on central subsidies are small ones recently graduated from the status of workers settlements, and large centers whose dominant industries are non-city enterprises, the profits of which go into all-union or republic treasuries.

deprived Soviet cities of their nearest equivalent of the real estate
tax that is a major source of revenue for U.S. cities. Statistics that
further break down revenue totals (by cities and sources) are difficult
if not impossible for Westerners to obtain. Cattell could find none
for Leningrad. Frolic reports that in Moscow only "ten percent of
revenues are levied by the municipal government."[16] Pertsik, a
Soviet scholar who reports on Irkutsk, concludes:

> Employing only local sources of income, local soviets
> cannot balance their budgets. However, in spite of the
> fact that regulated income is, in principle, distributed
> among local soviets each year, they remain dependent
> on higher soviets. This is the case because it is the
> prerogative of the higher soviet to determine the amount
> allocated. It is a fact that superior soviets do not always
> consider the interests of lower soviets when distributing
> the funds.[17]

The process by which a city's plan and budget are drafted rein-
forces its dependence. Since that process also contributes to the
formal separation of city from non-city agencies, it is treated in the
next chapter. Meanwhile two features of the bureaucratic framework
should be made clear. City soviets rely on higher authorities—for
advice and consent, and for money, materials, and manpower. Yet
in the eyes of its superiors, a particular city is only one of many
claimants on attention and resources, both of which, in a system
characterized by great size and extreme scarcity, are limited.

5

THE PUBLIC INTEREST
VERSUS THE PUBLIC INTEREST

Many American city officials like to depict themselves as courageous defenders of the public interest. Among their favorite targets—especially at election time—are "selfish private interests," such as industries accused of polluting air and water, of begrudging local taxes, or of transgressing municipal ordinances.

In the USSR, city soviets represent the public interest. But so do factories—the peoples' property doing the peoples' work.

City soviets, according to their formal mandate, coordinate urban development. They build and manage city housing and services, and local industries. They supervise non-city construction and operations in accordance with urban plans and legal norms. The first interest of non-city agencies is output—refining oil in an all-union refinery, digging coal in a mine operated by a regional economic council, making foreign guests feel at home (or homesick) in Intourist hotels, etc. Factory managers and workers are not paid to defend the city interest, but enterprise activities do influence the shape and quality of urban life. Industrial construction sets the pace and direction of urban growth, determining how much housing and services a soviet must provide. Construction of enterprise-owned housing and related services raises other questions: when and where are they built, and how are they to be maintained?*

---

*In 1960, 38 percent of all state-owned housing in the USSR belonged to regional economic councils and their enterprises, 30 percent to various ministries and state committees, and only 32 percent to local soviets. Of funds invested in construction of hospitals and clinics in the RSFSR in 1960, 35 percent came from councils and 45 percent from local soviets. For childrens' nurseries the

The opportunities for conflict are numerous. Balanced urban development requires cooperation between city and non-city agencies. Yet the rules that regulate their interaction have been, at least until 1971, as confusing as those concerning soviets and their superiors. Between 1957 and 1959 various republics adopted statutes to replace an obsolete 1928 all-union decree on local soviets (including province and district governments, as well as city governments). But only six (not including the mammoth RSFSR) adopted laws on city soviets, and those statutes were vague and conflicted with ministerial instructions concerning specific city departments.[1] "Render any assistance"; "take measures to control. . . ." Did ambiguity facilitate flexibility? Apparently not. City officials must know exactly what their rights are, wrote I. Azovkin, yet the statutes are "so inexact and so unclear that it is even difficult to consider them statutory."[2] According to Armenian Supreme Soviet Chief Arutunian, the laws "resolved few of the sorely pressing questions."[3] Other observers have concluded that "only a change in the situation . . . will permit soviets to influence their own enterprises more purposefully . . . and what is naturally much more complex, to influence industrial enterprises not subordinate to them."[4]

From the confusion of the law, one can attempt to outline the formal-legal relationship between city and enterprises. Given the record of soviet impotence, the picture seems somewhat surprising. For on paper, at least, cities possess formidable weapons with which to influence industrial agencies. On the other hand the formal relationship also includes imposing barriers to communication and cooperation.

FORMAL POWERS

Regional and urban plans, we have already seen, have often been distinguished by their absence or their shortcomings. More's the pity, from the municipal point of view, since effective plans could offer significant political leverage. Urban plans theoretically include detailed prescriptions for five to seven years, as well as a twenty-to-thirty-year forecast. They should stipulate city size, in territory and population; land use patterns, including residential and commercial

---

comparable figures are 58 percent and 25 percent. See I. Azovkin, "The Development of the Material-Financial Base and Competence of Local Soviets," Mestnye Sovety na sovremennom etape (Moscow: Nauka, 1965), p. 86. Statistics on housing and other municipal services in specific cities are given in case studies in Chapters 7 through 10 of this book.

zoning; scale, distribution, and character of industry, housing, and municipal services; street layout; urban redevelopment.[5] Most plans are prepared by central or province town planning institutes in conjunction with a city's chief architect and its department of construction and architecture. They are approved by the city soviet and (dual subordination) the State Committee on Construction and Architecture. Once adopted they are binding on all organizations, city and non-city.[6]

If there is any question about a city's ability to enforce compliance with its plan, its authority to allot land ought to be the answer— this being authority that should offer political leverage even to soviets whose cities lack formal, approved plans. No enterprise, agency, organization, institution, regardless of governmental subordination, can obtain land for construction without soviet permission. If an enterprise begins construction without authorization, the soviet may order a halt and also the razing of the site. If that order is ignored, guilty enterprise directors or other state officials are subject to criminal prosecution.[7]

A city may reclaim the land if construction does not begin on schedule. Once construction starts, city officials should see to it that the planned timetable is observed. They dispatch inspectors to building sites, and hear reports from contractors. When construction is finished, an acceptance commission is formed to inspect the results. The executive committee appoints commission members for all "public housing and other service buildings and facilities" regardless of who financed and built them. The city takes final responsibility by issuing an order "accepting the project," and penalizes those who use new buildings without permission.*

A similar pattern holds for operation and maintenance of enterprise-owned facilities. City soviets may issue ordinances, violation of which is punishable by fines, on the following subjects: preservation of public order; maintenance of housing and services; sanitation; preservation of forests, green areas and natural resources including air and water resources; public transportation; traffic; and collective farm market procedures. In case of factory violation, the manager, not the enterprise, pays the fine—a device designed to make a small fine hurt more and to circumvent the standard enterprise ploy of including "fine money" in the annual production plan. The city's administrative commission examines cases and imposes fines. It

---

*The purpose of inspections, both during and upon completion of construction, is "to check on quality and speed of construction and on organization of municipal services in the area, to ensure that conditions conform to duly affirmed plans, that technical norms are observed, and that the completed project will be suitable for use."[8]

may transfer serious cases to the police for criminal investigation.
Commission decisions may be altered or rescinded by the executive
committee, or appealed by a defendent to the courts.[9]

Housing gets particular attention in city government deliberations,
for, in addition to granting land, inspecting construction, approving
completed projects, and supervising maintenance, the soviet plays a
role in distributing new apartments. Municipal housing is distributed
by the executive committee.* In the case of non-city housing, enterprises choose tenants from among their own employees. Until 1965
city officials ratified enterprise lists of housing applicants, and in
addition received 10 percent of new housing space for general
distribution. But the 1965 economic reforms, designed to increase
enterprise incentives, decreased city access. No longer was the
soviet entitled to 10 percent, nor could it ratify enterprise lists.
Instead it would be "informed" of the names on the lists.[10]

Few rules could be more impressive in form and less in
enforcement. At best, many city governments have evaluated enterprise construction projects on narrow technical grounds rather than
demanding that all projects be, in the words of the central decree, "in
accord with plans for construction of the city as a whole." At worst,
enforcement of local ordinances has been so "flexible" (see episodes
in Chapters 7 through 10) as to amount to a charade.

STRUCTURAL BARRIERS

The most important barrier is the very process by which all
agencies (city and non-city) draft their economic plans and budgets.
This process is crucial for it sets each one's agenda and allocates
resources needed to fulfill assigned tasks. What impact can city
planning have unless it is coordinated with economic planning? What
force can a city ordinance have if it requires spending not authorized
in preestablished non-city budgets? To influence enterprises soviet
officials must reach them during the planning stage. Yet the process
is so structured that it offers almost no opportunity for formal contact.

Subordination and separation are the guiding principles—subordination of each local agency (city and non-city) to its superiors, and
separation of each from the other. Soviet budgets "are ratified from
the top down so that each soviet can approve its budget only after the
next higher budget is approved. . . ."[11] The city department of finance,

---

*In cities with borough subdivisions, distribution is by borough
executive committees which act, in this matter and in general, as
agents of the city executive committee.

which guides other departments and negotiates for the city with higher
authorities (at the province, republic, and all-union levels), is itself
a "dually subordinate" arm of the Ministry of Finance ("No one likes
us very much," was the way one finance department official put it"[12]).
Planning guidelines for municipal and industrial agencies come down
from on high (from the CPSU Central Committee and USSR Council of
Ministers in the last analysis), and local plans return there for ultimate
approval.

Separation really means isolation, for city and non-city agencies
do their planning and budgeting in their own bureaucratic hierarchies.
There is no formal provision for coordination at the local level. Unless
local agencies consult each other informally, the only body to coordinate their planning is their common superior, which, in the case of
the city soviet and all-union enterprise, is none other than the USSR
Council of Ministers itself! (For more details of the budget-plan
process, see Appendix B.)

What the budget-plan process means, in terms of bureaucratic
politics, is that city officials seeking to influence an enterprise must
worry about the enterprise's superior, a powerful industrial agency
that itself does not need to worry about most city officials and their
superiors. Suppose city leaders are inclined to divide and conquer—
to convince a ministry to pressure its enterprise, or an enterprise
to ignore its ministry. Then they must confront the fact of industrial
interdependence—that enterprises depend on ministries for planning
guidelines and resources; that ministries rely on enterprises to
overfulfill the plan and thus reflect credit on their tutelage.

That interdependence is an unseen joker in the 1971 Supreme
Soviet decree. The law says, in Article 3, that "city soviets hear
reports on the questions specified in this article [virtually all matters
bearing on urban welfare] by the executives of enterprises, institutions,
and organizations, adopt decisions on these reports and, when necessary, submit proposals of its own to appropriate higher agencies."
The law says, in Article 7(2), that the city government "examines
plans for the siting, development and specialization of . . . organizations
and institutions of culture, public education, and public health of higher
subordination, and, when necessary submits proposals to higher appropriate higher agencies." The law says, in Article 7(3), that the city
"examines those parts of draft plans of enterprises, institutions and
organizations of higher subordination located on the city's territory
that deal with the development of [housing and services] and, when
necessary, submits proposals to higher agencies." The law says, in
Article 7 (11), that the city executive committee "gives assistance to
industrial enterprises of higher subordination . . . and provides conclusions, which are subject to mandatory examination, on questions
involving the expansion of existing industrial enterprises, construction
of new ones. . . ."

The law giveth and the higher agency taketh away. That is why one must react skeptically to what is, on the surface, the most impressive article of all: the city soviet, when necessary, "suspends the implementation of orders and instructions, at variance with legislation, which have been issued by executives of enterprises, institutions, and organizations of higher subordination concerning questions of housing and services . . . land use, construction . . . and informs the appropriate higher agencies of such actions."[13]

Finding municipal cupboards bare, city leaders may covet a factory's resources; they may urge an enterprise either to build what the city needs or to transfer funds directly to the soviet. But since most factory resources are centrally allocated, soviet leaders who wish to dip into them may have to speak to the ministry.* Enterprises also possess funds from "non-centralized sources"—above-plan profits and savings. Enterprise incentive funds are designed to encourage local initiative (for example, by financing housing), but until 1965 they too were hedged about with central controls.[14] The 1965 reforms banned "withdrawal or redistribution of resources from the enterprise fund by the supervising agency."[15] Excessive central controls, wrote legal commentators, decreased the incentive that the funds are supposed to stimulate.[16] So had city soviet success in gaining access to the funds.** So would a scheme, long suggested by various city leaders but not established in 1971, for channelling a fixed proportion of incentive funds directly into municipal budgets. If soviets wanted contributions they would still have to bid for them. What could they offer in return—"flexible" enforcement of the law?

---

*Robert Osborn reports that in 1965, before the economic reforms took effect, "housing built from enterprise profits accounted for roughly 10 percent of the total paid for by state and enterprises together" (see Osborn, Soviet Social Policies, p. 226). All enterprise construction projects must be included in "title lists" approved by higher authorities. The statute on title lists, which identifies higher agencies approving projects of varying value, is Instruction of the RSFSR Ministry of Municipal Services, "On Procedures for Approving Title Lists for New Projects," February 13, 1963, cited in Andreevski, ed., Spravochnik, pp. 307-309.

**Excessive city soviet access "decreased the amount of housing belonging to the enterprises and thus lowered their incentive to achieve the high production indicators which expand the funds. The new system increases incentives in production and creates conditions necessary to attract new cadres." See P. Petrov and I. Ivanov, "The New Statute on the Socialist State Production Enterprise," SGP No. 1, (January 1966), p. 21.

In the face of America's urban problems, many liberal critics share Edward Logue's previously quoted lament that "the extent of public authority required" is "nowhere on the horizon," and that "we are not going to get it without some kind of crisis that will be painful enough itself so that we would all prefer to avoid it." What such critics wish for, what many are trying to invent, is some institution (perhaps metropolitan government or regional government) authoritative enough to pull diverse interests together in a coordinated attack on what ails the cities.

But while American cities struggle to invent a system for harnessing interests, Soviet cities seemingly have one—the Party organization with its first secretary, a sort of supermayor. To think of the first secretary in this way may require Western readers to reorient their image of the Party. The foundation of the Party's power is the fact that its bureaucratic apparatus parallels both municipal and industrial organs, and that Party cells penetrate these and other institutions in Soviet cities. Such are precisely the sort of arrangements that have given the Party its sinister reputation in the West. They were among the foundations of totalitarianism: thus the Party, it was said, controlled everything. Today the Party still seems ubiquitous—preaching the ideological gospel, laying down the political line, supervising the economy, mobilizing the masses. Yet the Party apparat spends a great deal of its time performing a necessary bureaucratic function that would seem almost prosaic if it were not so extensive; it oversees all suborganizations in the vast bureaucratic system; it coordinates their efforts in service of the public interest as defined by the high authority to which all are in fact, if not in theory, subordinate—the top leadership of the Communist Party of the USSR. When city and non-city agencies quarrel, disputes

could theoretically be settled without Party interference, either by
direct bargaining between rivals or through appeals to higher authorities. But a negotiated settlement could favor might not right; and
appeals to superiors can involve the latter in time-consuming deliberations too far from the scene to take local subtleties into account;
hence the city Party organization's mandate—"to direct all soviet,
economic, trade union and youth organizations, channeling all in one
unified direction."[1]

WHO GOVERNS THE GORKOM?

The city Party organization, like the city soviet, functions one
way on paper and another way in practice.[2] The Party conference
resembles the soviet session; theoretically a powerful deliberative
body, it actually ratifies and celebrates decisions made by its executive
branches. The Party committee (gorkom) includes important local
leaders in various fields, plus distinguished workers and (if there
are farms on the edge of the city) eminent peasants. The committee
(eighty-seven members and thirty-five candidate members in Leningrad)
is supposed to determine policy between conference sessions. But
often it serves simply as a sounding board for Party secretaries or
a forum "for assessing progress made by various administrative
personnel."[3] Real day-to-day power belongs to the Party bureau
(Moscow's had eleven members and six candidates), which includes
the mayor and certain non-city leaders, but it is dominated by Party
secretaries, sometimes by the first secretary alone.

Consider the composition of the Stalingrad province bureau:
between 1954 and 1962 the members of the bureau included the province
soviet chairman, the regional economic council chief, the trade union
head, the top security policeman, one or two key factory directors,
and the first secretary of the Stalingrad city Party committee. But
at all times the majority of members were province Party secretaries
and other apparatchiki.* Do city Party committees follow the same

---

*Ibid., pp. 89-99; 194-97. Stewart estimated the "potential
influence" of various province Party committee members. Group I
(those with the most potential influence) included—besides province
Party secretaries—the province soviet chairman, the regional economic
council chief, and the first secretary of the Stalingrad city party committee. Leading factory managers were in Group II, the mayor of
Stalingrad in Group IV. These ratings are interesting not only as a
pattern potentially applicable to city Party committees but also because
the province Party committee is a potential court of appeal for rivals
in city politics. (The groups listed in ibid., pp. 202-205.)

pattern? In Moscow in 1966 six of the eleven bureau members were Party secretaries; of "candidate members" identified, two directed Party departments and one was first secretary of the Party-controlled youth league. Similarly five of the Leningrad bureau's full members were Party secretaries, while the city soviet had one representative, the mayor.[4]

THE PARTY AND THE SOVIET

Party Rules instruct the gorkom to "lead" the soviet but not to "supplant" it. In 1957 a Central Committee resolution commanded Party committees to revive dormant soviets and warned against "interfering in administrative activities . . . [or deciding] . . . economic and other issues for them."[5] In 1965, another resolution cautioned Party authorities to avoid "trivial tutelage and unjustified interference in the work of soviets, to help soviets decide all questions in their jurisdiction independently [sic] and with full use of their powers."[6]

What distinguishes necessary guidance from unjustified interference? Party-soviet relations are "elusive . . . and difficult to specify."[7] It is not difficult to discover that a particular Party bureau has called in city officials for consultations or has demanded improvements in municipal administration.[8] But beyond that the published record is scanty. Cattell has calculated that, of the Leningrad executive committees decisions published in its bulletin, only about 8 percent were "directly inspired" by the Party in 1950 and 13 percent in 1961.[9] But one wonders about the significance of such statistics when one reads the candid admission of an "insider," the head of the Leningrad Party Committee's Department of Party Organs: "If you carefully examine the activities of local Party and soviet organs, then it is not difficult to be convinced that the most important decisions are adopted jointly, even when there is no written document involved."[10]

When there is no written document involved, there is the telephone, there are Party departments that parallel municipal ones, and there are primary Party organizations (PPOs or Party cells) in soviet agencies, which report to the city Party committee. Party cells are supposed to "promote improvement of the work of the apparatus, develop among employees a high sense of responsibility for work entrusted to them, take measures to strengthen state discipline and improve services to the public. . . ."[11] As Communists, leading executive committee members are subject to Party discipline from the gorkom.*

---

*Of all deputies elected to city soviet executive committees in the USSR in March 1965, 88.7 percent (15,476 deputies) were Party

Party and soviet leaderships interlock. The mayor sits on the
Party bureau, and Party secretaries sit on the city executive committee. (In Moscow the first secretary and two second secretaries
were ispolkom members in 1966; in Leningrad this was true only of
the first secretary.)[12] Clearly such seats give Party officials a voice
in the city policy, but how great a voice? Cattell reports that in
Leningrad "the primary means of Party control . . . is close personal
contact between Party and government, and a system of osmosis based
on long conditioning."[13] A Soviet dissertation suggests that similar
arrangements in smaller cities "give the Party committee a chance
to direct the daily activities of the soviet."[14] The first secretary of
a town of 50,000 people admitted that in such cities, where municipal
government is weak and understaffed, "we actually govern."[15] Nonetheless it seems unlikely that first secretaries dictate daily to the
executive committees of which they are members. Given their influence
over the hiring and firing of other members, they do not have to.
Party Rules give Party leaders the task of directing "the recruitment
and placement of cadres." That means each Party committee has its
nomenklatura—its list of city soviet jobs for which it selects or at
least approves appointments.

Just which city officials a given gorkom can hire and fire is not
clear to Western analysts.* But it is clear that shuffling people is as

---

members or "candidate members." Of all those elected to borough
soviet executive committees, 92.7 percent (4,066) were Communists.
In contrast, only 51.4 percent (118,591) of all city soviet deputies
elected in 1965 were Party members or candidates; for borough soviets
the comparable figures are 52.3 percent (42,881). For these and
similar statistics relating to soviets of other levels, see Sostav
deputatov mestnykh sovetov deputatov trudiashchikhsia izbrannykh
v marte 1965: statisticheskii sbornik (The composition of deputies
of local soviets elected in March 1965) (Moscow: Izdatel'stvo
Izvestiia, 1965), pp. 102-200.

*Frolic distinguishes among three "levels" of nomenklatura
jurisdiction. Top posts (mayor, deputy chairman of the executive
committee, heads of key municipal departments) are staffed "by the
city Party organization on the recommendation of higher Party and
state bodies." The actual extent of gorkom influence in these cases
appears to depend on "the type of post, the size of the city, personalities of those involved"; Party authorities in large cities have more
leverage, but by and large "the city Party organization still continues
to be dominated by higher authorities in the staffing of top municipal
non-Party posts." Middle level posts (top city bureaucrats and borough
leaders) "are staffed exclusively by the city Party organization."

important an activity as shuffling papers. Leningrad Party authorities transferred 140 former Party apparatchiki into the city government to revitalize it.[16] Dimitri Polyanski, later a Politburo member, was in 1957 first secretary of a province Party committee. He saw to it that 75 percent of local soviet chairmen were "former Party workers who went through a good school and can apply their experience." These were "proven and authoritative comrades" tested in Party work and trained by special Party institutes. Their transfer tested whether the troubles of local government were inherent in the offices or their occupants. The answer was soon apparent. The comrades worked "in such a way that the local Party organization must do their work for them. Of course, this is theoretically impermissible since the local Party organization should lead and not supplant the soviet. But often soviet workers' lack of initiative demands action . . . and the Party committee takes over again."[17]

THE PARTY AND NON-CITY AGENCIES

In theory the Party has more authority over non-city agencies than over the soviet. According to Pravda, local Party organs are supposed to lead (rukovodit') and direct (napravliat') economic enterprises in their territory.[18] According to Jerry Hough's careful study of industrial decision-making, the local Party committee acts as a "regional super-coordinator" with leverage inside individual enterprises and in interagency relations: the committee (1) verifies plan fulfillment and enforces legality; (2) acts as a court in departmental disputes; (3) studies the production process and recommends innovations; and (4) settles problems of supply and procurement by determining priorities.[19]

What weapons give Party officials such influence? Party cells offer inadequate access, since their mandate to monitor factory administration conflicts with the director's rights of one-man management. Much more leverage comes from Party authority over Party members, and from the nomenklatura. Actually these two levers are linked, for Party officials are more likely to pressure administrators whom they have appointed than those who owe jobs to a powerful central ministry or higher Party officials.[20] The nomenklatura is doubly indicative of Party influence, but outside analysts can only

---

Lower level posts (the vast majority) are filled by soviet agencies themselves in accordance with state regulations. See Frolic, "Decision Making in Soviet Cities," American Political Science Review, LXVI, 1 (March 1972), 48-49.

infer its contents from contradictory hints in the press. Sometimes higher authorities completely bypass city Party secretaries.* On the other hand some of the most important economic appointments, though made by ministries, are apparently cleared with city Party committees, and even nominations approved by the CPSU Central Committee are based partly on gorkom recommendations. Not just the powerful Leningrad gorkom, but borough committees as well apparently hire and fire important non-city factory managers. "We [the gorkom] dismissed" the director of a metallurgical factory on grounds of embezzlement.21 The manager of a 1,200-man woodworking factory "could not cope with his responsibilities and did not want to understand them, so we [the borough committee] replaced him."**

Like soviet leaders, city Party officials dealing with non-city enterprises must be ready to talk to the latters' superiors. Is the higher agency involved a ministry, or a regional economic council? The question was important because, under the ministerial system, local Party organs have both more to do and less influence than in the years when councils administered the economy. Under the ministerial system local Party committees are in effect the only regional coordinators (a job the councils were created to fill). Yet most city Party secretaries are not equipped to joust with ministers. In Soviet administrative theory (as summarized by Hough), "the interaction of a Party committee with a higher state official is not that of team decision-making, but rather a suppliant-superior relationship." A Party committee "can request that a higher administrative official take some action, it can appeal one of his decisions to a higher Party official, but it is not in any real sense an equal."23 Even the most powerful committees (both province Party committees and those in republic-level cities) are at a triple disadvantage: the Party secretary concerns himself with a given industry only part of the time, while the minister specializes; the minister is at the center of power in

---

*The Kiev Party gorkom nominates the director of the 2,000-worker Rosa Luxemburg Knitted Wear Factory. The Tbilisi gorkom nominates the director of a factory, which packs 25 percent of the tea consumed in the USSR. For these and other examples, see Hough, The Soviet Prefects.

**Two potential sources of Party influence are the power to investigate enterprises and control over the local press. But one finds no evidence that Party authorities use investigations to pressure enterprises on matters unrelated to the actual subject of the inquiry. And the local press seems to do much less muckraking than central papers do, whether concerning the sins of factory managers or of city officials.22

Moscow, while the Party secretary is on the periphery; local Party
secretaries have, with rare exceptions, less personal power and
prestige than important ministers.

Regional economic councils were easier targets, at least in the
years when council jurisdiction paralelled province boundaries.
Leningrad Party authorities moved, in various ways, to discipline
council officials. They rebuked one official for not requesting more
challenging production plans. They issued a Party reprimand against
another, apparently on the theory that the council would not feel
comfortable with such a sinner on its payroll. A borough Party bureau
issued a resolution calling for "strengthened leadership" in a council-
managed factory. Shortly thereafter the former director of the plant
visited borough Party offices; "why did you fire me?" he asked.24

Hough cites several cases in which Party officials forced
industrial enterprises to contribute money and materials to city-run
services. Such outside-the-plan activity, Hough concludes, "must be
considered irrational from the point of view of efficient operation of
industry," noting:

> But it is rational as far as the Soviet system as whole is
> concerned. Because of the inefficiencies of the planning
> mechanism, "above-plan" assistance from local factories
> may be the only way the regime's goals in agriculture,
> education, and adequate medical care can be met. In
> forcing enterprises to help all sectors in the region to
> meet the plans set by the center, the local Party organi-
> zations may only be correcting irrationalities which could
> not otherwise be avoided.25

That, a harried Soviet city official may be justified in saying,
is an understatement. For, despite the Party's supermayoral powers,
"irrationalities which could not otherwise be avoided" are not avoided
again and again, with painful consequences for citizens and even for
industry itself.

7

NEW CITIES:
THE POLITICS OF COMPANY TOWNS

More than a thousand new cities have been founded in the USSR since the Revolution, an achievement of which the Soviets are particularly proud. Industrialization has brought rural backwaters to vital urban life. But the process has left scars. One may expect new socialist cities to avoid the mistakes of the unplanned, pre-Revolutionary era. In fact they seem especially prone to poor planning and unbalanced urban development.*

Most new cities have been born and raised as Soviet-style company towns, in the shadow of one industrial establishment or with several establishments dividing responsibility or competing for control. The pattern was established in the 1930s. Central industrial ministries built not only factories but also housing and what meager services there were. City governments were an afterthought: they could do little more than ratify industrial actions—even when enterprises, concentrating on production, built insufficient housing and services, or when several enterprises refused to coordinate their efforts so that well-off factories had an abundance of services and poorer plants had virtually none. New cities grew so rapidly that,

---

*Between 1926 and 1969, 934 new cities were founded in the USSR. According to Soviet sources, new cities—and small cities (see Chapter 8)—are particularly vulnerable to housing and service shortages. But since Soviet writers deal in examples rather than systematic surveys, it is impossible to say how many cities exhibit a particular syndrome. The cases examined in this chapter are neither precisely representative nor completely random. Of necessity they are those about which most information is available. Soviet sources, from which virtually all information is gathered, describe them as broadly typical.

according to one Soviet planner, "plans served as illustrations not blueprints."[1] But even after new towns had become large cities, industries retained control. In an era of scarcity, factory managers learned to hoard valuable resources. Located far from older and more comfortable and cosmopolitan centers, they used housing to attract and hold personnel. In 1957—the year that reforms were decreed—managers still cherished the right to house their own workers (or not to do so if resources allocated for that purpose could be more profitably employed in the factory) and to evict those who left their employ. When city leaders broached the subject of transferring housing, services, and zakazchik rights, many managers reacted in traditional bureaucratic fashion. They resisted encroachments that would reduce their resources, dilute their prerogatives, and disrupt standard operating procedures. Accused of harming the public interest, economic administrators countered with the charge that city governments would be unable to cope with new responsibilities. Municipal administrations, they said, were inexperienced and inefficient; giving cities greater authority would harm industry without advancing the public welfare. What is more, some city leaders, good bureaucrats themselves, agreed. For them, new duties posed new challenges. Coping successfully could mean rewards sufficient to compensate for extra efforts; but failure could damage or disgrace. Would they receive sufficient additional resources to carry out new assignments? If so, they might be tempted to take them on. If not. . . .

Some municipalities accepted the challenge. But other local leaders preferred to let industry continue to rule. Some who shunned responsibility for themselves attempted to persuade industrial administrators to show more public spirit. But other city leaders, accustomed to powerlessness and inured to failure, continued as before.

The rest of this chapter is devoted to various case studies: first, cities where enterprising governments fought for their rights; second, cities where leaders did not seek implementation of the 1957 decrees; third, some of the Soviet Union's newest towns—founded in the 1960s—where lessons of the past have sometimes but not always been learned.

THE REWARDS OF ACTIVISM[2]

Magnitogorsk—Locus Classicus

Of all the new Soviet cities, Magnitogorsk exhibits most dramatically both the successes and costs of rapid industrial and urban

growth.* None was more celebrated for its feats of industrial production in the thirties (and during World War II the city's factories
produced steel for half of Russia's tanks and shells),[3] but in the sixties
no soviet was more frustratingly dependent on industry.

As the thirties began, the town in the southern Urals that was
to become world famous was a village of tents and ramshackle barracks; its inhabitants were workers preparing the blast furnaces
which would process the area's unusually pure iron ore. Ernst May,
a German town planner called in to work with Soviet planners, recalls
a controversy. Should the town be built on the right or left bank of
the Ural River? Lacking guidance from Moscow, and with construction
deadlines pending, May and his colleagues postponed the decision for
a while; they then began to build on the left bank, and finally took the
issue to industrial chieftains in Moscow.

"I decided on a tactic which I have frequently found effective,"
wrote May many years later:

> I had our draughtsman make a cardboard clock, with one
> hand, and labelled "Magnitogorsk." The hand could be
> turned to the left, pointing to the words "na levom beregu"
> [left bank], or to the right, to the words "na pravom
> beregu" [right bank]. The commissar for heavy industry,
> Orzhonikidze, who was responsible for Magnitogorsk,
> received me in audience. I handed him the clock and asked
> him to indicate with the hand the direction which I might
> then take as the final decision of the Central Soviet. With-
> out batting an eyelid and with a deadly serious face he
> turned the clock over and engaged me in a rather lengthy
> discussion of the advantages and disadvantages of each
> bank of the river, promising me a decision shortly. I
> never received it, but found out later that they had built
> Magnitogorsk on both banks.[4]

In 1960 the Magnitogorsk Metallurgical Combine, the mammoth
enterprise that dominated the city and its politics, owned 52 percent
of all state housing and operated most municipal services, including
the mass transit system; the Magnitogorsk Construction Trust owned
24 percent of city housing; and a calibrated gauge factory owned 8
percent. The remaining 16 percent consisted of "bits and pieces"
belonging to seventy other organizations, including the city soviet
(which had less than 2 percent).[5]

---

*Magnitogorsk was founded in 1932. Its population in 1970 was
364,000. It is a city of province (Cheliabinsk) subordination.

The large industrial enterprises not only planned for insufficient services but had not fulfilled their plans. The city's heating, water, and sewage systems were painfully inadequate. While large factories provided themselves with poor services, small plants could not afford any; their tiny housing projects—one or two apartment houses each—often lacked heat, water, and electricity. And the combine cut off electricity to homes whenever production required extra power— which prompted little girls skipping rope on street corners to sum up the politics of urban development in the following verse: "Na ulitse Lugovoi sveta ne imeetsia / Predsedatel' gorsoveta na lunu nadeetsia" (On Lugovaia Street the lights are out / The mayor has to rely on the moon.).[6] The combine cut off water too, without warning, for 30,000 residents at the hottest time of year—which may not have disturbed citizens quite as much as one would expect since the rest of the year water arrived in insufficient quantity from a pumping station dangerously close to a local iron ore enriching plant. Combine-operated transit was equally notorious; it desperately overcrowded because only 90 of 268 vehicles were on the street, while others awaited repair at the overworked depot. But the combine refused to allocate money for a new depot; meanwhile it was slow to include new schools and other institutions in its transit routes. Housing maintenance and sanitation were sore points too. Small enterprises lacked janitorial and repair staffs, while large concerns were over-staffed. Not even the combine had necessary machinery, such as garbage trucks, snow-removers, road-sanders, streetsweepers, and watering machines. The republic Ministry of Municipal Services could not help the combine; it could allocate such equipment only to soviets that ran their own services, a policy that encouraged cities to take over enterprise-owned facilities but penalized those that had not done so.

"I have been in Magnitogorsk," wrote a Soviet correspondent some years later:

> I remember one spring. Black streams flowed down black slopes, while the hard-working city suffocated in an ag-glomeration of fumes. The commendable, prizewinning, etcetera, etcetera Magnitogorsk Metallurgical Combine throws off a monstrous quantity of sulphur dioxide in these fumes. If this quantity were calculated in terms of sul-phuric acid, it might constitute a considerable percentage of the country's total sulphuric acid production! Animals, plants and the soil suffer; buildings deteriorate before their time; clothing is ruined; and even metal does not last as long as it should. Flowing into the rivers with the rain and spring floodwaters, the sulphur compounds contaminate

the fish and diminish the already diminishing number of sources of drinking water. Who has taken all this into account? And, most important, what is the monetary cost of the actual losses arising from people's lower working capacity?[7]

What had the city soviet done to remedy these ills? Had it invoked its formal-legal authority? Had it arranged for small builders to pool their efforts, or for large and small to cooperate so that no house would be without necessary services? Had it insisted on such joint measures as a prerequisite for land allotments? Had it enforced ordinances setting standards for maintenance of housing and services? Had it called in higher state officials to act against polluters?

Pooling construction funds of small builders was impossible; such builders had no funds to pool, and it was apparently considered a waste of time to appeal to their superiors for increased allocations. Municipal authorities had encouraged cooperation; allotting land to the combine, the city retained 10-15 percent of each plot for small builders in the hope that they would link up with the water, electricity, and sewage systems of the giant enterprise. But the small landlords had to petition endlessly while the combine usually found various excuses for not cooperating. "Almost every time," recalled a city councilman, "the executive committee had to get involved, trying to prove to the combine that its narrow departmental approach damages the city interest."[8]

Rather than threatening sanctions, city officials had accepted enterprise excuses. The central fact of Magnitogorsk politics was the soviet's dependence on industry. Threats would antagonize managers on whose goodwill so much hinged (even though that goodwill was often distinguished by its absence). Levying fines against polluters would only alienate them—unless the polluters had been thoughtful enough to include "fine money" in their annual economic plan; in which case the soviet could have a steady source of income, the enterprise would not begrudge the outflow, and only the environment would suffer.[9] Before the city could think of moving decisively against recalcitrant enterprises it would have to reduce its dependence on them. One way to do that might be to seek transfer to the city of factory-owned housing and services.

Magnitogorsk could not count on automatic implementation of the 1957 decrees, nor had it felt free to appeal directly to republic authorities for action. Instead the city had asked enterprises for their approval and for suggestions about how the transfers should be handled. The director of the combine, a key figure in the talks, rejected the city's proposal as "incorrect." He defended his construction record as "well planned and efficacious," charging that the city was

attempting "to smash" the existing order, and predicting that giving
power to the soviet would produce poor housing conditions for combine
workers. The construction trust agreed to transfer its limited service
facilities but not its housing. Housing attracted workers and kept
them, said the director, who was supported by officials of the factory's
Party and trade union committees; the trust would fight to retain its
right to evict workers who were fired or took jobs in other plants.[10]

Extended negotiations followed—for three years. City officials
insisted that the combine's efforts did not deserve the name of "planning," and they gave the label of "an empty excuse" to the directors'
claim that their right to evict was the prime source of labor force
stability. That might have been so in the past, but in 1960 recruitment
had virtually ceased and, in any case, improved working conditions
and workers' morale were enough to ensure "constant cadres." The
mayor assured combine and trust that the last thing he wanted was
to disrupt industrial work forces. After all, "the ispolkom could not
but realize that metallurgy was the dominant occupation in the city,"
and only an insane city leader would hinder its operations in any
way.[11] To prove its goodwill, the city offered to let the combine
continue to distribute apartments in housing it transferred to the
soviet; the executive committee asked only for the right to inspect
lists of new residents, a right that, according to law, it should have
had even before any transfer. Instead of demanding immediate transfer of zakazchik authority for new construction, the city offered to
wait until the end of the seven-year plan in 1965. But the enterprises
made no concessions.

During the negotiations the city Party committee supported the
soviet.[12] The Party first secretary must have taken his stand despite
opposition from important industrial spokesmen on the Party committee. But the Party committee could not decide the issue because
the combine invoked the aid of its superior, the Cheliabinsk Economic
Council. After that the city's only recourse was to appeal to the
Cheliabinsk Province Executive Committee.[13] But since neither
higher agency could dictate to the other, the stalemate continued.

Next the city complained to the Ministry of Municipal Services,
the agency that would supervise city-owned services whenever
Magnitogorsk managed to obtain some.

"Why haven't you helped our city," Magnitogorsk Mayor Antipin
had asked.

"Which city?" the Minister replied.

"Why Magnitogorsk, of course."

"But there is no such city," said the Minister. "Your city is
not a city. It is the property of the metallurgical combine which used
to be subordinate to the Ministry of Ferrous Metals and now works
under the Cheliabinsk Economic Council."[14]

Having done with his little joke the Minister agreed to help. But unfortunately he could not act until authorized by still higher authorities. Such a knot could only be untied by the republic Council of Ministers, the common superior of both province soviet and economic council. The Council of Ministers examined the controversy (while at the same time Izvestiia and Sovety deputatov dramatized the Magnitogorsk soviet's plight) and finally announced its decision: to delay final decision until after the combine had built a new transit depot and had improved the water-supply and sewage systems.[15]

What happened after the Council of Ministers had spoken? In 1970 a new mayor of Magnitogorsk discerned "a certain amount of progress." Retail stores had been transferred to the city; so had public baths. After five more years of "negotiations" the city had obtained a municipal gas trust, a construction trust and a modest sanitation department. "Nonetheless," the mayor continued, "Magnitogorsk remains what it was ten years ago—a company town [gorod pri zavode]," a town where four major enterprises owned 65 percent of the housing; a city where the combine-controlled water supply system was still insufficient, but where a new reservoir-connector was in its fourth year of construction while industrial projects costing many times more were completed in much less time; a city where combine-run transit still produced endless citizen complaints that the soviet could not act upon; a city where factory managers and their ministerial superiors "for some reason still do not seek close relations with the city government."[16]

Novokuznetsk—Strong Mayoral Leadership:
Its Impact and Limits*

In 1957 the mayor of Novokuznetsk was Pavel Ivanovich Oturin, a resident of the city since 1933, formerly its chief architect, and a corresponding member of the USSR Academy of Construction and Architecture. A vigorous defender of the city interest against what he called "the special interests," Oturin believed that "our city is old enough to care equally for the production plan, and for the living conditions of its citizens."[17] Oturin's prestige and his forceful use of soviet authority won the city some victories. But the mayor and his successors could not sustain the pressure, and though battles were won, the war, apparently, was not.

---

*Formerly called Stalinsk, the city is referred to throughout this account as Novokuznetsk. It is a city of province (Kemerov.) subordination.

Metallurgy made Novokuznetsk, too. From a village of 3,000
in 1929, the city (founded in 1931) grew to 168,000 in 1937, 400,000
in 1959, and 499,000 in 1970. But while industry built the city, no
one effectively planned its growth.

"First there appeared the mines and factories," recalled Oturin,
"and, then around them, the residential areas. No one knew which
enterprises were coming; no one planned for a sewage system, roads,
green areas or anti-pollution devices." In the early days the river
served as sewer. When city authorities appealed for help, they felt,
recalled Oturin, "like Don Quixote tilting against windmills."[18]

In 1957 Novokuznetsk reflected its past. The Novokuznetsk
Metallurgical Combine owned nearly half the housing, while more
than a hundred other enterprises owned the rest. Various non-city
agencies maintained water-supply, sewage, and electricity systems,
and even owned streets. As usual, housing and services lagged behind
industrial growth.

A road construction problem particularly galled Mayor Oturin.
The main route to the south led through the center of Novokuznetsk.
The executive committee had long urged construction of a bypass,
but could not afford to build it. The city had the legal authority to
assign enterprises to road construction, but local factories, backed
by their superiors (most recently the Kemerovo Economic Council)
refused. When the council began construction of a new plant, Oturin
acted. The council, without consulting the soviet, sent heavy equipment
across the city to the plant site. Oturin, without consulting the council,
barred such equipment from city streets as a health and safety
hazard; if builders wanted to reach their site, they could build the
bypass. Council administrator leaders were reportedly "amazed"
to receive such a "categorical nyet"; the project, they warned, could
not wait. "There was a hot argument," a report continues, "but
finally they understood Oturin correctly in the council and in other
province organizations. The by-pass will be built."[19]

Oturin discovered that three large industries spent less than
half the funds allocated to them for nonindustrial construction; the
metallurgical combine spent 47 percent, a coal trust 45 percent, and
the Kuznetsk Aluminum Factory only 11 percent. Strictly speaking
this was a matter between the enterprises and their superiors. But
Oturin tried to persuade them to increase outlays. He called the
soviet into session to exert public pressure.

"Why do you talk about millions if you don't spend them?" a
deputy asked.

"How can you say you know the needs of the population?" demanded
another.

"Let Zheriabin [director of the metallurgical factory] answer
one question precisely. When will you build schools, a hospital and

laundry in the Togolino settlement? And another thing. The houses
have fifty separate boilers which pollute the air with smoke. All you
have to do to prevent that is to link up the houses with a central
boiler. Why don't you solve that?"

"It does not take millions of rubles to haul away garbage and
fence off and protect the lawns," reproved a fourth speaker. "It
takes only some awareness of your responsibility. We don't need
more phrasemongering, comrades; we need more service from those
who have obligation to the city."

Criticism had an effect. "Not everything was done, but there
was an improvement."20 But the big enterprises still stinted on
garbage collection, and continued to do so even after Oturin called
a conference of enterprise housing administrators, their janitorial
supervisors, and city health officials. Oturin invited the combine's
deputy director, M. I. Argunov, for a stroll amid uncollected refuse.
Argunov accepted but did not appear—which happened not once but
several times, each time Oturin waited in vain in the street. When
at last the combine official did appear, Oturin accused him of indif-
ference to the city's welfare in such strong words that Argunov
declared himself insulted, left in a huff, and failed to appear at an
executive committee meeting called to discuss the whole issue. What
was to be done? Drop the matter, leaving the combine to flout a city
ordinance? The mayor asked the administrative commission to act;
it punished Argunov with "a month of compulsory labor at his place
of work." The decision "was like a bolt of lightning from a clear
sky to him and it served as a warning for others. Now they know
there are angry men on the ispolkom."21

The fact that Argunov received the news of his punishment with
such astonishment indicates how little he expected it. Clearly, the
city had not used such tactics often. Nor did it in the future. For
fundamental problems persisted, as a team of Izvestiia reporters
discovered in 1961.22 Housing was still divided among 150 different
enterprises, the largest of which were not fulfilling their construction
plans.

"Imagine an industry which fulfilled only 50 percent of its plan,"
Izvestiia demanded. "Is housing a second class item? Of course
not. But for the metallurgists it is. Their main job is producing
steel."

The city soviet, whose main job should have been housing, built
no houses in 1961. "It has no goals, no money, no materials," said
Izvestiia. Nor had it a voice in distributing new apartments. Enterprises argued that their own control procedures sufficed: "Every
shop gets its fair share," said the combine's chief of housing and
services, A. A. Alekseev. But Izvestiia discovered that, in one new
apartment house, all eighty apartments had gone not to the shops

but to leading managerial personnel, with Alekseev himself getting
a particularly choice flat.

Enterprises guarded their independence like sovereign states,
and they refused to aid their neighbors. The scene on one block was
so reminiscent of balance-of-power politics that it became known as
"International Street." For five years enterprises had debated whose
territory new water pipes would cross—while houses nearby did without water. City-owned electrical cables ran to central connecting
points; factories argued about whose wires extended from there. The
city government played the same game: municipal snow-removal
machines sat idle rather than work on "foreign [i.e., industrial]
territory."

The situation was absurd, said Izvestiia. Enterprise spokesmen
agreed in theory, but nonetheless successfully fought the transfer of
housing and services.

"Create a city-managed construction trust? Transfer money
and materials? Why you must be joking!" said one manager. "It's
much too early for that. In Moscow and Leningrad things are different.
Here, we must wait."

Some managers, like the above-mentioned Alekseev, offered
elaborate but disingenuous proofs of their organization's virtue.
Others, like the deputy director of the Western Siberia Metals Trust,
were more candid: "You know," he said, "when you have your housing
and your own housing staff, you feel a little more comfortable somehow. And remember we do not turn anyone away when they need
help. Just let them come and ask."

"But what if you were in your neighbor's place," Izvestiia had
asked, "How would you like, as they say, to have to 'pay your
respects'?"

"I?" The manager laughed. "I would start our own independent
housing program."

Could the soviet handle new responsibilities? Enterprise officials "scornfully expressed their doubt." Izvestiia disagreed. Its
correspondents asked Alekseev and the municipal housing chief to
calculate how much each spent on capital repair. The wealthy combine, it turned out, skimped on housing, spending only ten rubles per
square meter in 1960 while the soviet invested thirty.

This demonstration proved dramatically, Izvestiia concluded,
that the city could and should do more. A 1965 report revealed some
progress.23 But in the same year, when the economic council was
disbanded, its zakazchik powers were transferred not to the city but
to new ministries—which proceeded to spend even less on services.
In 1968 a new Novokuznetsk mayor echoed his Magnitogorsk colleagues' ten-years-later-not-much-better lament.24

THE BETTER PART OF VALOR

Factory managers charge that cities cannot run housing and services efficiently. Does municipal management really mean a lowering of standards, or does transfer simply deprive enterprises of their right to satisfy their own employees first, and to neglect them when production demands top priority?

According to the USSR Central Statistical Administration, local soviets (including province and district, as well as city) manage housing more efficiently, more profitably, and with more concern for residents' welfare than do non-soviet agencies.[25] On the other hand the press is filled with stories about cities which misspend housing funds.[26] New cities, by their leaders' own admission, must proceed cautiously in assuming responsibility. When some city governments hesitated to seek implementation of the 1957 decrees, the natural question—asked in the press—was whether their leaders were being sensibly realistic or inexcusably slothful.

Kramatorsk—Sensibly Realistic

Kramatorsk, founded in 1937, has 151,000 inhabitants (1970) and is a city of province (Donetsk) subordination. Writing in 1965 the mayor of Kramatorsk recalled articles on Magnitogorsk that had appeared five years earlier. Kramatorsk too, he noted, had "grown up around several mammoth factories—machine-building, metallurgical and others—and our ispolkom also had no opportunity to manage city affairs, to influence the direction of growth during pre-war construction, and post-war reconstruction."[27] In 1965 the city government was still struggling for influence, but it had not sought transfer of enterprise-owned facilities. Kramatorsk, said its mayor, was not rich; it could not be compared with the well-to-do province capital, Donetsk. Instead of depriving industries of their non-industrial assets, Kramatorsk urged them to build more.

According to the mayor, the situation had recently improved to the point that no important problems were settled without the executive committee's participation. If so, the gain reveals more about past impotence than present power. The mayor still could not prevent enterprises from ignoring the city interest: a new plant without pollution control devices defiled the air from its first day of operation; wealthy enterprises declined to contribute funds to city-operated recreation areas and stores. Nor could the mayor influence agencies that seemed to forsake their own interest—for example, the Ukrainian State Planning Commission, which, in funding a new casting and forging plant, included no housing and services. Some managers, said the

mayor, "see only the economics of production. They understand that
clearly; they speak about that with great warmth. But ask them in
what conditions people live and work, and they will not be able to
answer."*

The power to allot land offered no leverage against an enterprise
that did not even bother to report new construction. When the plant
was completed, without anti-pollution devices, the mayor asked why.
"The director shrugged his shoulders," the mayor recalled. "There
was nothing more to say. It was too late for the city soviet to change
anything."

The city needed enterprise help to maintain municipal facilities—
the beach, movie theater, stores, parks. To ask for aid was embar-
rassing, but as the wags at city hall put it: "He who doesn't knock
will never be admitted."

"We knock," wrote the mayor. "As loudly as we can, on factory
doors."

But even he who knocks is not always admitted.

Enterprise director: "We'll be glad to spruce up around the
factory. We'll find men and money for this somehow. But the city—
that's far away from us. That, pardon me, is none of our business."

Mayor: "Pardon me, but everyone knows that factory workers
live throughout the city, that their children go to various schools,
that their wives shop in widely separated stores. And what about the
city beach, movie theater and parks? Don't workers of all factories
visit them?"

Three times the city appealed to the Ukrainian State Planning
Commission to build services along with the new casting and forging
factory. The replies, the mayor said, suited the 1930s, not the 1960s:

"You'll manage somehow."

"Everything will take care of itself."

"The people who built Magnitogorsk lived in tents—and look
what a miracle they created!"

Angarsk, Electrostal, Krivoi Rog—"We Cannot Do It!"

Angarsk, founded in 1951, has 204,000 inhabitants (1970) and is
a city of province (Irkutsk) subordination. Its population increased

---

*From another source comes a story of how the director of the
New-Kramatorsk Machine-Building Factory clashed with his own
workers. They asked the enterprise to repair a footpath that many
took to work. Rather than fix it, the director, without warning, blocked
off the path with a brick wall. The workers complained both to the
city ispolkom and to Izvestiia. See A. Dolenko, "The Case of the
Factory Path." Izvestiia, May 10, 1962. p. 3.

fivefold in its first ten years. During the same period the municipal
bureaucracy added one slot.28 In 1960 non-city enterprises monopo-
lized housing and services, which lagged behind industrial growth.
But when Angarsk officials did not seek transfer of these facilities,
Izvestiia charged dereliction of duty: "The shyness of the city government can be explained only by their liking for the peaceful quiet life.
Why should they, they say, take on such a heavy burden? Why should
they worry about municipal services? Let things go on as they are.
Let the enterprises suffer with the burden."29

The only way to begin, said Izvestiia, was to begin, and city
officials heard the same message when they asked the Ministry of
Municipal Services to authorize a municipal gas trust. "Your city is
not a city; it belongs to the enterprises." The joke was now standard
operating procedure at the ministry. "That is why we cannot create
a city gas administration. After you take over enterprise housing,
then we will see what we can do."

Thus prompted, Angarsk officials finally requested transfer of
housing, and also funds and men to run it—only to find their original
fears realized. Province authorities temporized; they understood
the problem, they said, but had to explain it to their republic superiors.
The economic council, apparently angered by the city's demands,
discouraged its enterprises from extending further aid to city projects.

Electrostal, founded in 1938, has 123,000 inhabitants (1970) and
is a city of province (Moscow) subordination. In Electrostal, said
Izvestiia, the soviet leaders' motto was "We cannot do it," an opinion
with which the newspaper reluctantly concurred.30 Enterprise-run
services were notoriously inefficient and the mayor wanted nothing
to do with them. Said Izvestiia: "In a city of industrial giants, where
enterprises have resources and funds, the city, quite frankly, does
not do very much and that has a debilitating effect."

Krivoi Rog, founded in 1926, has 573,000 inhabitants (1970) and
is a city of province (Drepropetrovsk) subordination. In Krivoi Rog,
city officials were so discouraged that province and Party authorities
had to step in and virtually govern. Industrial enterprises acted,
reported Sovety deputatov in 1960, like "separate principalities."
But the soviet exerted hardly any pressure for change. Its requests
for reform was so halfhearted that enterprises felt free to ignore it.
And no wonder factory managers were uncooperative. Many city
bureaucrats were simply incompetent; the deputy commissioner of
municipal services, for example, did not know how many public baths
the city had, or where they were, or even who was in charge of them.31
Party officials issued such detailed instructions that "half the time
the soviet was actually repeating what had been done by Party organs."
Each time city leaders sent a request to factory managers, they also
sent copies to the city Party secretary who they hoped would act as
"enforcer."32

Cases like these hold different lessons for different observers. Industries react by tightening their grip on their housing and services. But partisans of reform seek a place to begin. Izvestiia, while condemning incompetence, endorsed change nonetheless—or rather precisely because local governments were inefficient. Only an injection of new authority, though perhaps unsettling in the short run, could energize the soviets. And in the long run, they, and not the industrial enterprises, were best qualified to govern cities.

"Up to a certain point," said an Izvestiia editorial, "it makes sense" for industries to guide the construction of cities; after all, factories are "naturally concerned about the life of their workers." But once the village of Magnitogorsk grows into a large city with a variety of enterprises and institutions, "it stands to reason that the metallurgical combine, whose job is producing steel, will be unable to run city services effectively." Continuation of enterprise control stunts the soviet's growth and saps its morale. "Master of the city in theory, but possessing authority without resources, it is not master in fact." When cities seek more responsibility, enterprises ask: " 'Will they be able to cope with it? Have they the capacity and the funds ?' " Izvestiia answers: "Of course, they will manage, as long as the resources which enterprises now spend on housing and services are also transferred to the city."[33]

THE NEWEST CITIES

"There are two schools of thought," wrote Pravda's correspondent:

The first says: Begin by creating normal housing conditions for the workers; provide necessary consumers' services; build roads and electric transmission lines; lay water mains, etc. Then start regular oil production.
The second school says: The main thing is production. Everything else is subsidiary. Normal living conditions can be created while oil is being drilled. In time, the contrast between production and the quality of life will be eliminated, and everything will be put right.[34]

Pravda's subject was the new towns rising at the sites of Siberian oil and gas deposits. Its correspondent described Gornopravdinsk, which was founded in 1964 and developed by adherents of the first school. To the objection that balanced urban development was difficult in "Siberia, with its impassable taiga and swamps, where even clay is transported by air," the geologist-founder of Gornopravdinsk

replied "Precisely! Here as nowhere else we must be concerned
about housing and services to compensate for the burden imposed by
Siberian conditions."

Was Gornopravdinsk unusual? Apparently so. "The proponents
of harmful, one-sided development have taken no heed of its example,"
reported Pravda. "They still sing the same old tune: Gornopravdinsk
was an exception. It is only a small settlement pop. 2000. Experi-
mentation is possible there, but just try to do the same in Surgut!"

Paucity of sources prevents one from making blanket generali-
zations, but the following cases (described in the press as typical)
suggest a pattern. Like their 1930s predecessors, new cities of the
1960s have grown up as company towns. But in the sixth decade of
Soviet rule some city officials take their formal mandate seriously,
cite the Party's propaganda for balanced development, appeal for
help in the press, and sometimes win their way.

Apatity

Apatity was founded in 1965 when two settlements in the mineral-
rich Kola District of far-northern Murmansk Province were merged
by a vote of the RSFSR Supreme Soviet. At the time, four agencies
and enterprises were active in the area: the Apatite Combine, the
Academy of Sciences, the Kola Geological Administration, and a
hydroelectric station.[35]

The procedure for forming the city government is revealing.
First to be created was the city Party committee, and only after that,
the executive committee. Party and the province officials sought a
suitable candidate for mayor; they chose V. E. Bessmertnyi, chief
engineer of a local ore-enriching plant. At first, Bessmertnyi refused: the factory needed his attention (the director was away for
an extended period); he had no knowledge of local administration;
and, besides since few people in town knew him, he might not be
elected ("Such things happen sometimes," he said). But his benefactors
insisted, he finally accepted, and the soviet session dutifully elected
him.

From the start the mayor found himself at odds with his neighbors. Lacking street-cleaning and snow-removal equipment, the city
asked enterprises to be responsible for certain assigned streets.
"Somehow or other and not very quickly," mayor and managers
reached agreement. But the jobs were "more easily assigned than
done, and some streets quickly became known as "orphans." When
enterprises failed to live up to their agreements, Bessmertnyi waited
several days ("for the dough to settle," he said), then inquired about
the delay.

"All our machines are busy on construction work," was the answer. "Either construction or street cleaning—we have to choose."

Chagrined, the mayor marshalled his forces. He consulted city Party officials, then the police, health, and sanitation inspectors, and the administrative commission. The law, he said, must be enforced "without making any deals": "Let them all understand that we are building a new socialist city. We are the master here, and not the guest. We are responsible for anything that goes wrong."[36]

The strategy worked. The academy's representative had "an unpleasant explanation" at Party committee offices, then agreed to cooperate. The administrative commission convinced the combine. Sanitation inspectors fined several other factories.

But victories in street cleaning did not produce cooperation in construction. Agencies planned houses without roads; persuaded by the mayor to include services, the builders left them for last. Asked why, enterprise representatives waved "a life-saving piece of paper." "You see," a combine official explained, "the Ministry of Chemical Industry approved the title list without stores or a communal kitchen. That's what the ministry decided. What do you want from me?"

"You should have consulted with us before sending your application to the ministry," the mayor replied. "We know the city's needs better than the ministry does. Let the ministry re-examine its decision."[37]

Did city officials really expect to force a ministry to change its mind? Or did they suspect that the enterprise had made the controversial decision, which the ministry simply ratified? The latter would seem likely, for, once the combine was persuaded to change its mind, the ministry agreed as well.

The mayor threatened to deny future land allotments unless projects were built as planned. When the hydroelectric station delayed construction of a health clinic in a new residential area, the mayor would not accept poverty as an excuse: "Several thousand of your workers live near this project. Where are they to be treated? No-where! You cannot build houses without a clinic. If you delay further we shall take away that plot of land and give it to some other organi-zation. I would advise you to worry about finding funds before it is too late."[38]

What gave Mayor Bessmertnyi the courage to act so boldly? Had Party and province authorities promised extra support when he agreed to become mayor? Were his victories any more lasting than those of Mayor Oturin of Novokuznetsk? Would city leaders eventually face retaliation from enterprises on whose cooperation so much depended? Or would gains be protected by higher authorities who had learned some lessons since 1957? Pending further press coverage (or a most unlikely Intourist-sponsored visit), one cannot say.

The New Towns of Tiumen Province

The assault on the oil and gas riches of Tiumen Province in
western Siberia is being launched from "three lines of communities":
rear-echelon industrial bases in Tiumen, Tomsk, and Tobolsk; a
second line of cities planned for 100,000 population—among them,
Urai and Surgut; and a third line of "small compact settlements"
conveniently located near oil and gas fields.

Second-line cities were the subject of a Pravda investigation in
March 1970.[39] "The urban plan," said Pravda, "should be the foundation of foundations—the law; without it, construction of a city cannot
begin—no more than one can build plants, mines, dams or roads without a plan." But not in Tiumen Province. There, urban planning was
"in a state of chronic lag." Plans which should have been drafted in
province design bureaus were stalled in overworked, understaffed
central institutes. Meanwhile "the oil people, the builders, and power
station people cannot wait. The gushers, they say, are their life
blood."

Too many companies spoil a company town. Instead of coordinating construction to make "a single ensemble," each agency builds
its own—"bathhouses, makeshift bakeries, canteens and commissaries,
heating plants, and what are aptly known as 'dives'." Some structures
are in a style known locally as "traditional temporary," but other
barracks, ironic monuments to technological progress, will be hard
to tear down. "Just imagine trying to tie all these projects together
with a single network of municipal services," sighed Pravda.

In Urai, founded in 1963, with population of 18,000 in 1965, the
mayor had tried to do just that.[40] The town was the creation of the
USSR State Committee on Oil and Gas Industries. The city government
was the state committee's stepchild. The result, according to Sovety
deputatov, was the following:

> The city has neither a water supply nor a sewage system.
> With the exception of a small prospectors' settlement,
> the town was not landscaped. Next to the barracks are
> uprooted stumps, construction refuse and other garbage.
>
> In Urai there are fourteen stores. But what stores!
> Small, inconvenient. Each saleslady serves 500 customers,
> on the average. Try to be polite under those circum-
> stances! Stores and cafeterias open at seven a.m. and
> close at eight in the evening, although most of the oil
> workers leave for work at six in the morning and many do
> not return until nine or ten in the evening.
>
> In the whole city there are but three small cafeterias,
> seating altogether 150 persons. It is not surprising that

> there are lines at lunch time . . . or that food is not tasty,
> or that the staff has no time to keep the place clean. . . .
> At the very least, Urai needs five or six more cafeterias.
> In Urai public baths there are 30 places; people must
> wash where they can.
> Each enterprise decides what and where to build.
> Each opens its own library, club, hostel. But all are
> dwarfish. In Urai there is neither a real library with a
> good reading room, nor a club where one could call a
> meeting for a large collective or arrange an evening for
> youth.[41]

Despite these problems the city received minimum support
from its superiors. The district and province blamed the oil interests.
But Sovety deputatov's correspondent charged that the province soviet
seemed "inexplicably calm," that it did not "confront the offending
organizations with the chaos in Urai," and that it "did nothing to save
the newborn city from its lonely neglected existence."[42]

The deputy chairman of the RSFSR State Committee on Construction (Gosstroi) told Sovety deputatov that his committee answered
only for construction of province capitals and other large industrial
centers. He said his committee's only task in smaller cities was to
define "technical policy."

"Now pay close attention," was the journal's reply:

> Gosstroi RSFSR defines the technical policy in city con-
> struction. But what happens when people do not follow
> this policy, when they grossly distort it? Is it conceivable
> that Gosstroi does not care how its general line is imple-
> mented? That, as we all know, is exactly what happens, as
> the story of Urai demonstrates once again. In Tiumen
> Province, agencies build new cities . . . according to an
> unwritten rule: to each his own. But that doesn't even
> give the leaders of Gosstroi a headache: the technical
> policy is defined—after that, the deluge.[43]

Sovety deputatov challenged higher agencies to explain their
actions. Five months later the journal described the response:
Gosstroi's State Committee on Civil Construction and Architecture
had dispatched inspectors. Together with province officials, the
visitors had set guidelines for construction in Urai, as well as in
Surgut, Nefteiugansk, and Nizhnebartovsk. A session of the province
soviet had discussed the shortage of services. A new bus service
had opened in Urai.[44]

Less than a year later, Surgut's mayor complained to Sovety
deputatov. He did not know "whether higher organs had kept their
promises about Urai, but as far as Surgut was concerned there has
been no improvement." The city "still suffers from the very same
ailments as a year ago."*

---

*Quoted in P. Munarev, "Must a City Be Born in Torment?" SDT,
No. 1 (January 1967), p. 33. A city of 17,000, Surgut stretched more
than ten kilometers—because non-soviet enterprises built where they
pleased. Usually the builders did not provide municipal services; when
they did include these, their superiors deleted them from plans. The
city badly needed new schools, stores, clubs, and roads. Intended to
become the home of 200,000 people, Surgut offered its present residents
"a mass of inconveniences."

In July 1967 Izvestiia published an open letter of complaint from
a Russian Supreme Soviet deputy (Tiumen Province) to heads of the USSR
Gosstroi, the Ministry of Gas Industry, and the State Construction Bank
(A. Protozanov, "Temporary Building or Permanent Apartment House?"
Izvestiia, July 13, 1967, p. 3). Their replies directed his attention to
"the realistic possibilities of the national economy," and assigned
responsibility for urban planning to the reluctant RSFSR Gosstroi.

In January 1968 Pravda summoned representatives of agencies
active in Tiumen and confronted them with evidence of urban neglect.
They denied responsibility for some problems, promised to rectify
others (see I. Titov, "Cities Rise in the Taiga," Pravda, January 8,
1968, p. 3). In March 1970 Pravda published the lack-of-progress
report cited above.

8

THE SMALL-CITY
SYNDROME

Difficult and persistent as they may be, are the problems of new industrial boom towns preferable to those of small, less industrialized cities? Unbalanced development is unfortunate, but is underdevelopment worse?

"There exists the opinion," reported a province Party first secretary, "that only capitals and large cities are entitled to all municipal conveniences while as for the rest of them—well, let God look after them."[1]

Those whom God looks after receive less support from their Soviet superiors. According to formal Soviet statistical usage, small cities are those of under 50,000 population. There were more than 5,000 such cities in the USSR in 1968, constituting 93 percent of the total number of cities and containing 50 million people. Medium-sized cities range in population from 50,000 to 100,000. But the small-city syndrome is a widespread condition affecting more than just the under-50,000 towns. According to small-city officials, the crucial distinction is between province capitals, which are privileged, and lesser cities, which, whatever their size, are not.

Half the industrial output of the RSFSR is produced in seventy-one province capitals.[2] Small and medium-sized cities provide consumer services at a per capita volume as low as one-twelfth that of large cities.[3] To leaders of small cities, province centers appear twice blessed: industries build housing and services (which for all their faults appear attractive to a city which can afford few services of its own); in addition, the state supplies extra subsidies. The rich, it appears to small-town Russia, get richer. As Robert Osborn puts it, "The Marxist principle, 'to each according to his work,' has been applied to communities as well as individuals."[4]

Patterns of politics differ in three kinds of small cities—
province-level communities (that is, subordinate to province soviets)
with fairly extensive industry; district-level towns (subordinate to
district soviets) with some industry; and small, district towns with
virtually no industry at all.

PROVINCE-LEVEL CITIES

In contrast to new company towns, older cities possess their
own municipal housing and services. In a sense they inherited the
situation that the 1957 changes were designed to achieve. The result,
however, is not independence from industry, but rather a different
kind of dependence—precisely the dilemma that some new-city leaders
feared would accompany implementation of the 1957 decrees. Small-
city soviets run services inefficiently—partly due to insufficient central
subsidies, partly as a result of local incompetence. Seeking assistance,
city leaders appeal to enterprises, which, though they do not dominate
as in new cities, nonetheless possess valuable resources. The soviet
that accepts handouts—funds, materials, technical aid—becomes
beholden for favors in return. On the other hand factories may refuse
to help, preferring to hoard scarce resources rather than to seek
special treatment from what they consider to be an irresponsible
city administration.

Of small but older cities of province subordination, Zlatoust
is said to be typical. Subordinate to Cheliabinsk Province, Zlatoust,
founded in 1754, is a city of 181,000 inhabitants (1970).[5]

A Sovety deputatov correspondent interviewed key political
figures—the director of the Zlatoust Metallurgical Plant and the
heads of several city departments.

The director levelled certain charges against the soviet—
charges that, in new cities, soviet officials direct against enterprises:

—Trade: City stores are too few and irrationally spaced. Store
hours are arbitrary and ignore workers' needs. Unscrupulous sales-
men sell vodka illegally to employees on their way to work.

—Laundry and dry cleaning: There are but one or two establishments in the metallurgists' district. Workers waste time travelling
to the center of town.

—Water supply: The city-run system supplies water irregularly
and unpredictably, in some places early in the morning, in others late
at night. People conserve water in pails, and he who is not home on
time does without.

—Transit: Trams run irregularly. At rush hours they cannot
cope. Extra buses for the factory district would help, as would a new
road. Meanwhile, workers must leave home very early and "take the
trams by storm."

In sum, said the director, the shortages "ruin workers' morale and lower their productivity."[6] Sovety deputatov's correspondent agreed. But who was responsible? The tram system had not been expanded in thirty years, during which time the population had doubled. Built for 50 cars, the old depot now handled 120. "They sewed the jacket for a baby who has since become a man," was the way the city's transport administrator put it. But province authorities would not authorize construction of a new depot.

City officials were also responsible. They excused themselves by pointing to a lack of funds, and promised to do better. But they did not make the small but important improvements that, according to the correspondent, would not cost a great deal of money.

The enterprises complained about city facilities but did not help. In 1965 the mayor asked a central ministry to include a food-store in ministry-financed housing then under construction. The response was an "ultimatum: either the housing without a store or no housing at all." After strenuous persuasion by the soviet, the ministry retreated. But when the city asked for funds to expand other services, Moscow threatened not to build any more housing in Zlatoust. And this particular "war", said Izvestiia, was "not unique."[7]

Other cities, similar wars. Piatigorsk (founded 1830; 1965 population, 77,000; a city of province—Stavropol—subordination), said Izvestiia, was the scene of "clashes between special interests and city interest and a host of unnecessary arguments."[8] The special interests employed unusual tactics. Instead of ignoring the soviet—the classic pattern—factory administrations resorted to "sounding the alarms, ringing all the bells, and accusing municipal officials of conservatism and other deadly sins." The mayor sounded his own alarm, complaining about the enterprises in a letter to Izvestiia.

Bedriansk authorities, sinned against, they said, by their superiors as well as by enterprises, were also divided among them-selves. Bredriansk, founded in 1835, had a 1969 population of 84,000; it is a city of province (Zaporozhe) subordination.[9] What was the soviet doing to enforce its will? Why did it not employ its legal powers? The city's chief architect replied: "Powers? Who pays any attention to them, especially in cities like Bedriansk?"*

---

*Among non-city agencies' alleged transgressions were the following: (1) The city's plan envisaged transfer of a shoe factory beyond the city limits; the regional economic council built the plant in the city. (2) A cable factory built a water-supply station on the beach, but reneged on its promise to landscape the area. (3) A construction trust, requesting city permission to build a workers' rest home on a spit of city land, promised to erect pleasant two-story structures. It built ugly one-story barracks.[10]

What was the reaction of higher authorities to the soviet's appeals? "Peter passes the buck to Paul," said the architect. "I, as chief architect, ought to ring all the alarm bells, and I try to do so. But our little alarm is not heard in Zaporozhe or Kiev. We write, we receive answers, we file them away. . . ."*

Within the city government the architect took a hard line toward the enterprises. He wanted, he said, to "hit them with the ruble." But the mayor, more sensitive to the possibility of retaliation, favored reprimands and warnings.[12] Did the architect feel he was accomplishing anything? He remarked: "Of course we are achieving something. We succeed in a few things. The city has a plan. It is growing, improving; the resort is being built. The real point is that things could be even better."

DISTRICT-LEVEL TOWNS

In district towns, officials sometimes sound as if things could hardly be worse. Of all soviets these have perhaps least leverage on their own superiors; hence they are particularly vulnerable to industrial domination, or, even worse, to neglect. Such towns are at the bottom. Their petitions must travel farther to reach the top. Their appeals must be approved by more superiors, each of which weighs competing claims of many local governments. Their immediate superior is the district soviet, which, since its primary concern is agriculture, can be insensitive to urban problems and needs. Yet district towns usually lack a full complement of municipal departments and therefore must rely on the district's bureaucracy, as well as on the city Party committee.

Aiaguz, a Kazakhstan city of 35,000 founded in 1939, exhibited all familiar symptoms in 1958.[13] The water-supply system (belonging to the Turkestan-Siberian Railroad Administration) was in a particularly poor state. The pipes, laid twenty years before, had not been extended, while the population multiplied four times. People living

---

*Among soviet grievances against higher authorities were the following: (1) The city appealed for help in moving railroad tracks which ran along the sea front. Ministries said they were not against the move if the city paid for it. According to the architect, "Everyone knows that a city like ours does not have the resources." (2) The province soviet, denying funds for a district boiler, forced the city to build new houses near a factory with a boiler—resulting in unwanted dependence on the factory and an undesirable extension of city limits.[11]

on the edge of the city had to walk as much as three kilometers to obtain water from public faucets. But the railroad pronounced its needs "satisfied," and the province could neither spend soviet money to repair non-soviet pipes nor afford to finance a new municipal water system.

The railroad's stores, which served mainly railroad personnel, operated on schedules timed to the trains. The district soviet's trade network stocked city stores with goods that had sold poorly in the countryside. When the city requested a municipal trade trust, higher authorities (the province soviet and the Ministry of Trade) attached the label "municipal" to the same stores—a move that, according to the mayor, changed nothing.

The city Party committee's word carried little weight with the province and republic governments. The Party and soviet appealed to the Kazakhstan Council of Ministers to expand the electricity network—ten small non-soviet systems producing current at a prohibitive cost. The republic government took the matter under advisement, and kept it there indefinitely.

The Ministry of Municipal Services said its first task was "to take care of Semipalatinsk," the province capital. When Aiaguz discovered that Semipalatinsk had not spent 50,000 rubles of its allocation and asked for 20,000 of that sum, province authorities retorted that Aiaguz was greedy. Not so, said the mayor, and the province should know it.

Mayor I. Levishchev's complaints to the press produced some action. The Kazakhstan Council of Ministers reprimanded all higher agencies, ordered Semipalatinsk Province to take corrective measures, and commanded various republic ministries to draw up a long-range plan for the city, to build the new electric station, and to supply money and materials for other projects.[14]

The airing of one city's problems encouraged others to speak out. Officials of Karataly (founded in 1944; 1965 population, 36,000; in Cheliabinsk Province) echoed Levishchev: constant skirmishes with the railroad, bad relations with a district soviet, and unsuccessful appeals to province authorities.[15] Similar complaints followed from Stepniak and Novoukrainsk.[16]

In 1967 came the turn of the chairman of Gagra, a city of 25,000 inhabitants (1965), founded in 1933, and subordinate to the Abkhaz Antonomons Soviet Socialist Republic of the Georgian SSR.[17] Moscow-based resort administrations dominated his Black Sea coast city. When hotel managers begrudged funds to maintain city streets, "no one supported us . . . and nothing was done." The city "could not move a step without permission of the district soviet." But the latter, which controlled the city budget and siphoned off its above-plan income, failed to rally to its support. Said the mayor:

Strange as it may seem the city soviet has no rights. It
cannot influence construction. It adopts ordinances . . .
and . . . has the right to bring violators before the administrative commission. But it has no such commission.
They tell us to use the district soviet's commission and
be satisfied. But what happens? That body is so overloaded with affairs of rural and settlement soviets that
in 1966 they did not examine even one violation of a city
decision.

One must not think that the ispolkom did not appeal
to anyone on all these questions. We knocked on the door
of the district organizations and leading organs of the
Azbakh ASSR and the Georgian SSR. We appealed, we
cited evidence, we noted the example of the Sochi City
Soviet. But they shrugged: "You have more than enough,"
they said. "Why Sochi, that is a big city; but all you have
is 25,000 people."[18]

Consider Kamennogorsk, a city of 15,000 inhabitants (1970),
founded in 1940, and subordinate to Leningrad Province. "Municipal
services stagnate while industry expands," wrote the mayor of
Kamennogorsk in 1968. "In that contrast one can see the enduring
view of the small city: 'It will manage somehow, but others are
more important.' But small cities have big problems and they are
getting worse all the time."[19]

SMALL-DISTRICT TOWNS: INDUSTRY WANTED

There are about 1,500 small cities, each with a population
of less than 50,000, which have no industry, though many
of them have long been in need of industrial development
and a complete material and spiritual renewal. The
development of small cities would solve many important
and extremely acute social, economic and city-planning
problems. The point here is not just the fate of cities
themselves. The small city that renews itself enhances
and transforms the entire surrounding district.[20]

Some of these towns arose as regional garrisons in Tsarist
times. Others were relics of early industrialization. Per capita
spending on housing and services in 1966 amounted to between 60
and 65 rubles in a sampling of such towns, compared with 172 in
Moscow.[21]

Official government policy, at least in theory has been to
stimulate small-town growth, both for their sake and to brake the
big-city boom. The Twenty-Third Party Congress reaffirmed that
policy in 1966. The State Planning Commission compiled a list of
500 towns "with favorable prospects for industrialization," towns
along railroads or waterways, and towns with "considerable labor
resources."[22] The situation is doubly ironic. Industry, with its
dubious record as tutor to new cities, is invited to care for another
set of orphans. But instead of taking up the challenge, ministries
shun it. For the fact is that industries do not relish governing cities
any more than city soviets like them to; they prefer to expand in
large cities where the existence of housing and services saves them
the expense of building their own.

In this, as in their opposition to other urban reforms, powerful
industries have generally not bothered to justify their behavior in
public. But, increasingly in the 1960s, some Soviet writers did so.
Labor productivity and return on capital are higher in large cities
than in small ones, argued V. Perevedentsev. "While maintenance
of a person in a very big city does cost more than in a medium-sized
one . . . in a big city, each person's output is greater."[23] The 500
towns designated by Gosplan "will not undergo industrial development
in the next few years," while for the rest of them—towns with under
20,000 population but with a total 10,000,000—"industrial growth is an
unattainable dream. It is not even pie in the sky; it is Shangri-la."[24]
If they listened to Perevedentsev, small towns would be content with
a more modest lot—offering service to rural consumers, education
for farming youth, and rest and recreation for big city dwellers.

Perevedentsev is not popular among orthodox planners.
Ministries, they say, may prefer large cities, but the cost of municipal
services "increases in geometric proportion as excessive enlargement
of the city proceeds." Industries may not consider that fact, but city
governments cannot avoid it. The debate goes on.[25] And meanwhile
small-town politics centers not around conflict with industry but in
campaigns to attract some. One town's story is instructive.

Kozmodemyansk (Kuzma, as it is known by its 13,500 inhabitants)
will be 400 years old in 1983.[26] Ivan the Terrible camped on the site
overlooking the Volga on his way home from a military expedition to
the south. In the nineteenth century the town was an important layover
point for Volga boatmen moving timber down the river.

As of 1965 no public buildings had been constructed in Kuzma
for forty-eight years. The town's most impressive structures—former
homes of nineteenth-century merchants—housed the school, clinic,
and cinema. Other buildings were flooded each spring as water
rushed through city streets to the river. Kuzma industry was the
local variety—a cannery, a small dairy, a brickyard and, in a belfry

built in Peter the Great's time, a kerosene shop. Automation had so
thinned the ranks of timber men, that many able-bodied workers spent
winters in Gorky, Volgograd, or Kazan, returning in the spring to
grow crops they would sell in the cities in the fall. Young people
were leaving Kuzma in search of vistas that the local school had
opened but the town could not deliver.

A nearby town, Ioshkar-Ola, had been more fortunate. Selected
as capital for the Marii Autonomous Republic, its population had
spurted from 89,000 in 1959 to 166,000 ten years later. It had been
rewarded with new enterprises, housing, and services. Meanwhile
"Kuzma became utterly superfluous and quite forgotten. Left to eke
out its own existence, the unhappy place had been relegated to the
category of 'small town.' And so time came to a halt in Kuzma."

The search for industry, however, did not. For one thing, Kuzma
had to resist Ioshkar-Ola's attempts to appropriate certain paintings
for the capital city museum, and to close Kuzma's theater so as to
apply money saved to its own. Kuzma's protest to Moscow against
the "theater grab" only succeeded in delaying it. Meanwhile the
mayor tried to attract industry. He appealed at Party conferences
and soviet sessions. He sent emissaries to the regional economic
council and to Moscow. He sought "equality," or at least "attention."
He was accused by those he pestered of "manifesting localist self-
interest."

Finally the province Party authorities changed their mind and
decided to look over Kuzma. Townspeople watched from their windows
and held their breath as the visitors, guided by the mayor, toured the
town. The committee recommended building a new hydroelectric
station. Its proposal was approved. Construction plans included
housing and services. "The attitude to small towns will change now,"
wrote a correspondent. "It is already changing, and they will no
longer be forsaken."

Perhaps. But in the meantime, small-town spokesmen continue
to envy province centers. And this raises the question of whether the
latter are worth envying. Have they achieved balanced growth in ways
which new and small cities can hope to emulate? Do capital city
officials possess the influence and independence that others attribute
to them?

9

POLITICS IN
PROVINCE CENTERS

It is said by leaders of new and small cities that province centers are privileged. Such centers own more housing and services than do new cities. They receive more attention and support from higher authorities than do small cities. Logically then, they should be less dependent on industrial agencies; in fact enterprises could even be dependent on them. If so, province center officials should be more willing and better able to fight for balanced urban development.

Capital city leaders are indeed more influential than those of, say, Chervonograd or Magnitogorsk. But province centers exhibit familiar symptoms and some special problems of their own as well. Urban governance is a more equal political struggle, but a struggle nonetheless.

The most obvious symptom is excessive urban expansion, often in defiance of legal restrictions.* As usual, industries have been largely responsible (or irresponsible), caring little if their expansion

---

*Where relevant, 1970 population figures for cities discussed in this chapter are cited in the text in parentheses after first mention of each city. Among those with particularly striking population growth patterns are Novosibirsk (from 404,000 in 1939, to 1,161,000 in 1970, compared with a planned 1975 total of 850,000); Kuibyshev (from 390,000 in 1939, to 1,047,000 in 1970, compared with 700,000 anticipated for 1975); Gorky (from 644,000 to 1,170,000 compared with 840,000). A 1960 Soviet source on the planned totals for 1975 is cited by Timothy Sosnovy, "Housing Conditions and Urban Development in the USSR," New Directions in the Soviet Economy, Part II-B, Joint Economic Committee Subcommittee on Foreign Economic Policy, U.S. Congress, 2nd session (Washington, D.C., 1966), pp. 533-53.

81

strains city-owned services. But in some cities, soviet leaders are also involved—refusing to oppose industries and often actively encouraging them.

"With the exception of enterprises necessary for direct services to the population, the construction of new industrial enterprises and the expansion of existing ones is at present prohibited in 34 cities of the Russian Republic. . . ."[1] This rule was promulgated in December 1969. But where industrial and city officials join to circumvent the law, professional city planners have no choice but to allow for industrial growth in long-range urban plans. Economic plans for 91 RSFSR cities (including 68 province centers, but not Moscow and Leningrad) project a 250-percent increase in industrial output by 1980, adding 2,700,000 industrial jobs plus about 600,000 new service positions. Due to a shortage of workers in these cities, urban plans have to provide for resettlement of 7,400,000 persons from other cities and rural areas, in addition to the natural population growth of about 3,500,000. Prohibition against industrial construction is no obstacle; in fact the population growth will be proportionately greater in cities where industrial expansion is restricted than in those where it is not. To keep pace, "an enormous upsurge" in housing and service construction will be needed, but (in the understated judgment of one Soviet observer) "the plans do not provide economic substantiation for the outlined growth in the population of cities: the total volume of capital investments necessary for implementation of a vast complex of work on . . . industrial facilities and city services is not determined, and the size of losses connected with expansion of built-up suburban agricultural land is not calculated."[2]

Why do city leaders, apparently breaking with their own architects and planners, go along with industries? Because capital soviets are not so privileged after all; because they, too, receive insufficient support from superiors and therefore count on enterprises for aid—for contributions to city projects from enterprise incentive funds, for housing and services potentially transferable to municipal control, for (indirectly) the extra attention and resources that Moscow may be willing to devote to a rapidly growing industrial center. Industries seeking to build in large cities offer in compensation what one province official called "mountains of gold." But when the factory goes into operation, the official continued, "everything is forgotten; construction of community facilities, street repairs and other improvements are all put off from year to year."[3]

Collecting compensation is the soviet's problem. Industries have the freedom to deliver or not, or to deliver only in return for further favors—irregularities overlooked (in construction or maintenance), or soviet acquiescence in additional expansion. Factories need not pay the city for extending utilities; they owe neither extensive taxes nor a fixed percentage of profits. Compared with new cities, province centers have been fairly successful in obtaining transfer of enterprise housing, services, and zakazchik rights. But with these gains has come a frustrating new dependence on superiors who attach so many conditions to their allocations that even as zakazchik the city soviet cannot plan effectively.

One way to reduce dependence on industry may be to compel factories "to share the cost [of their expansion], to compensate the city in full. . . ." The soviet would "collect differentiated payments for use of fixed assets (water, gas, electric power lines, roads, urban transit, housing, schools, medical institutions)."[4] To reduce dependence on superiors, city leaders have pressed another campaign—for greater flexibility in spending centrally allocated funds. Meanwhile the province centers suffer from a vicious circle: higher authorities supply insufficient resources, which compels city officials to beg aid from enterprises, who demand favors in return, which the soviet grants, which makes city leaders malinger or be dishonest, which convinces higher authorities their parsimony was justified.

LVOV—THE ADVANTAGES AND DISADVANTAGES OF BEING A PROVINCE CAPITAL

In the early years of reconstruction after the Great Fatherland War (1941-45), planners gave first priority to industry. Factories built their own housing, and then they quarrelled about who should provide electricity, roads, and sewage systems. Lvov (553,000) encountered what one province official was later to call "the most complex question of local administration: how to overcome the selfish approach to construction of services," how to get around the fact that "the interests of city and enterprises do not always coincide"?[5]

Some enterprises changed their ways. In 1961 they agreed to transfer zakazchik power to the city soviet. They trusted city authorities to act fairly and efficiently.[6] Enterprises were apparently satisfied, but city officials were not. After 1961, central funds for nonindustrial construction were still allocated, in the first instance, to industrial ministries, then channelled—through the USSR state Planning Commission, Ukrainian Gosplan, and the Lvov Province Executive Committee—to the Lvov City Soviet. The process took several months; by the time it was completed, the deadline for providing construction contractors with official documentation (September 1 of the year before construction begins) was usually past.[7]

Why such a cumbersome procedure? Why continue to allocate funds to industrial ministries? Why then channel them through republic and province authorities? Although the role of the ministries is not spelled out in Soviet sources, an explanation does suggest itself. Although they no longer finance construction directly, ministries may wish to use their status as source of the funds in order to make claims on use of the finished structures. Would they not, in any case, resist relinquishing title to substantial resources whose diversion from their direct control may prove, with a little effort, to be only temporary? As to republic and province authorities, they participate in this bureaucratic minuet as superiors to the city soviet. As such they channel all centralized funds destined for the city; they go so far as to designate funds for specific municipal projects, and may even perhaps skim off some for their own use or for diversion to other places. Soviet officials in other cities have campaigned, as we shall see, for funds without republic or province strings attached. Lvov officials proposed bypassing industrial ministries, a reform for which they were still pressing in 1968.

Cooperation between the city and enterprises developed in other areas. The soviet, even as zakazchik, lacked funds; it requested enterprise aid. But unlike soviets in new and small cities, Lvov could contribute resources of its own. On that basis, enterprises were willing to help; in fact they were pleased not to have to construct their own facilities. Together, city and non-city agencies built (1) a clinic in a factory residential district, (2) an extension of a water supply system badly strained because enterprises used up to 30 percent of the city's drinking water for their industrial needs, (3) 70,000 square meters of streets and sidewalks, and (4) new electricity lines and heating plants.

Not all, of course, was harmony. Enterprises continued to finance housing with incentive funds, and some insisted on shortchanging services. Once, city officials managed at the last minute to persuade a factory to erect a laundry in a remote corner of its new apartment house complex. "Now people complain to us about the location of the laundry," wrote Mayor A. Iagodzinskii. "It does not comfort them very much to learn how hard we worked to convince the factory to build any services at all."[8]

But other enterprises asked for advice in investing their funds, and some even went so far as to invite the soviet to spend them itself. Leaders of smaller cities dream of such an arrangement, but Lvov officials encountered objections from superiors. Not that higher authorities advised looking a gift horse in the mouth; the problem was that centralized procedures were too rigid to accommodate last-minute local generosity. The State Planning Commission allocated equipment— more dear than money—for municipal projects without taking enterprise offerings into account. Construction contractors were reluctant to take on incentive fund-financed projects, because (1) they received more material from their superiors for centrally financed work; and

(2) they received 10 percent of all apartments in centrally financed housing and none in incentive fund buildings.

"Clearly the factories and the soviet know their city's situation better than higher authorities do," declared the mayor in 1965. "Why, then, are they barred from allocating funds as they see fit?"[9]

In the aftermath of the 1965 reforms, enterprises offered even more money, which the city could not legally accept.[10] In the fall of 1968 Mayor Iagodzinskii protested again in Izvestiia.[11] Denied permission to accept enterprise gifts, he accepted them illegally. He described the elaborate charade:

> What happens next is known to all: one must hide the 'illegally' spent funds as far as possible from the eyes of the inspector. If they discover a violation of financial discipline, then there will be no end of unpleasantness.
>
> Many an ispolkom and soviet resort (as we do) to mobilizing enterprise money for the daily necessities of the city economy. It has become a tradition. It often is taken as a manifestation of initiative deserving all kinds of praise. As a matter of fact we hardly think it strange anymore to push enterprises into circumventing the law. One must admit that there is great moral irony in this.

Besides moral irony there were "a multitude of obvious absurdities." Particularly disturbing was industry's habit of building more plants and attracting more workers, while letting the city worry about services for them. In 1965 the mayor had complained that "drafts of factory construction are not cleared with the city soviet, a fact that makes things very difficult for us." In 1968 the soviet still sounded, Iagodzinskii said, "like a voice crying in the wilderness."

To make matters worse the province soviet had begun to manifest "a certain lack of confidence" in city government. Province authorities had reduced city staffs, and taken over municipal gas, lighting, and road-repair trusts. Needless to say, said the chairman, these changes "have had an ill effect on city life." They deprived the soviet of "the leverage needed to be master." They were turning the executive committee into something small-city leaders would recognize; the mayor said himself—"a suppliant."

KUIBISHEV—VICIOUS CIRCLE IN A PROVINCE CAPITAL

City officials in Kuibishev (1,047,000) have apparently been less successful than those in Lvov. Their record is hardly one that small-city soviets would wish to emulate.

Instead of helping Kuibishev to become zakazchik, the province
soviet assumed that power itself. The 1957 decree was implemented
only on paper, while the province permitted all the familiar evils to
continue. Small non-city builders, Sovety deputatov reported, "went
their own capricious way," each insisting on a piece of land in the
city center, few willing to join together in city-sponsored projects.[12]
Large builders were even more arbitrary; in one famous case a
metallurgical factory tore down 900 ten-year-old homes, even though
empty land was available nearby; only after an angry expose in
Izvestiia did the Kuibishev Regional Economic Council reprimand its
underling. Province officials permitted enterprises to begin construction without the city architect's permission; when the city appealed to
the procurator's office, the latter took no action.

Sovety deputatov reported in 1961 that city officials were despond-
ent. Pained by their superiors' behavior, they hesitated to request
zakazchik powers in fact as well as name. "They took it away from
us only a year ago," said one official, "so they are not likely to support
us now." But beneath the pessimism, the correspondent thought he
detected a more disturbing malaise: perhaps the Kuibishev leaders
were "afraid to take on responsibility for housing construction in the
city."[13]

Sovety deputatov's revelations produced action. Province authorities agreed to help establish a municipal department of capital
construction.[14] The province Party committee moved to "strengthen"
the city government by changing personnel—a former city Party secretary was made mayor; a former borough secretary was made deputy
mayor—and then by backing up the new appointees. Aware of his
mandate to guide but not "supplant" the soviet, the province first secretary had done what he called "some businesslike prompting: the
managers were reminded that the soviet and its executive committee
are organs of state power and that their directives are binding on
all."[15]

By 1965 the city had obtained the staff needed to act as zakazchik.
But, said Izvestiia, unreconstructed managers regarded the city's
new authority as "inconvenient," and continued to seek "autonomy."[16]
Using incentive funds, and even central funds supposedly now allocated
to the city, each manager built "his own housing, his public baths, his
laundries, barbershops and movie houses"—all at minimum cost.
Three large concerns even got the city to acquiesce in a repetition
of the 1961 scandal. The three (one was the same metallurgical plant)
obtained land on which were located 800 fairly respectable one-story
homes, although nearby was a district of decrepit barracks that badly
needed razing. Why did the mayor not object? Izvestiia has explained:
"The trouble is that the executive committee depends a great deal on
enterprises in the city. Thus, for example, four huge factories in

Kirov Borough own more than a million square meters of housing.
The factories' housing and service offices take care of services and
repairs. That is why, ignoring the best interests of the city, the
ispolkom permits enterprises to build what they want, where they
want."17

Not only did the city depend on enterprises to keep their own
districts in order; it also sought help for city facilities. It had no
choice, wrote Mayor A. Rosovskii, because the soviet's superiors
provided insufficient funds and materials.18

Consider the problem of housing repair. The RSFSR government
supplied funds and materials according to certain norms. The norms
were woefully inadequate, and were not even met: "We received only
a quarter of the norm in paint, whiting and oils, and they did not give
us any steel armatures at all. They tell us to find these materials
locally. This 'recommendation' is difficult to fulfill. And so, in the
end, we repair the foundations and the wall, but not the water pipes."
Even less satisfactory was the system for repairing service facilities:
"For these, the planning organs allocate only one eighth the gas tubing
that they do for apartment houses, and only one tenth the roofing and
slate. The people at Central Services and Supply usually tell us to
depend on local resources. And that means we must live on enterprise
handouts [emphasis added]."

True, there were some enterprises that contributed willingly and
without conditions. "Oil money" helped finance schools, kindergartens,
hospitals, and stores. Other factories helped build a trolley car depot
and maintain roads. But when agencies refused to cooperate, the city
was powerless to influence them.

The irony of the situation was not lost on the mayor. Enterprise
managers and journalists might criticize the city government, but the
mayor indicted the system:

> If this situation existed only in our city, then one could
> blame the ispolkom. . . . But, unfortunately, matters are
> the same in other province capitals. In fact, it is one of
> the paradoxes of planning that one agency's gain does
> direct damage to the general economy.
> How to remedy the situation?
> The city economy must be put on an industrial basis.
> It must be guaranteed necessary funds and material
> supplies; and in addition it needs a powerful mechanized
> construction-repair base, fully equipped services,
> transport, etc.

In the centralized Soviet system, only higher agencies could
supply these necessities, said the mayor, but to do so, they must have

a change of heart: "Local soviets cannot solve these problems themselves. This is an all-state question and can only be solved as such.
[Higher soviet organs] must rid themselves of the prevailing view that
municipal services are some kind of third-class matter."*

KHARKOV AND KRASNOIARSK: GOSPLAN IS THE VILLAIN

In Kharkov (1,223,000) and Krasnoiarsk (648,000), city officials
considered themselves trapped between ungenerous superiors and
favor-seeking enterprises. But both soviets had special grievances
against republic planning authorities.

In 1957 Kharkov's mayor had sounded as depressed as Mayor
Khripko of Chervonograd: "We are virtually powerless to resolve
many questions of city life . . . and the service of our citizens." The
trouble was a multiplicity of zakazchiki. "Try under these conditions
to locate shops and services in places most convenient for people.
All attempts run into barriers of special interests."19

By 1965 the city was zakazchik for centrally financed housing
and service construction. But in June of that year a team of Izvestiia
investigators reported that new residential districts showed the same
defects as old ones: houses were completed without necessary services, schools, and stores; heavy construction equipment had to return
to complete the job, at great cost to the city and with noise and
inconvenience for residents. With the city as zakazchik, what
prevented more coordinated construction? Izvestiia's detailed answer
deserves to be quoted in full:

> Extreme centralization of planning in housing construction
> inhibits the city executive committee. The Ukrainian State
> Planning Commission and republic ministries allocate
> funds to the executive committee, designating them for
> construction of specific houses, schools, hospitals, stores,
> etc. All expenses are outlined on top, even including how
> much to spend on the foundation and how much on the roof.

---

*The chairman of the Kiubishev Province Soviet Executive
Committee agreed that the city needed more funds but declined to
provide them. He suggested that the soviet receive a percentage of
non-city enterprise profits, put that money into a fund for municipal
services, and do so formally and regularly, so that the grants would
be the soviet's by right and not by begging. See V. Vorotnikov, "Local
Soviet and Enterprise," Izvestiia, August 1, 1968, p. 3.

Even inside a given residential district, the executive committee has no right to maneuver funds and materials.

For example, let's say that the interest of the city demands that a club be built instead of a school or a store. We repeat—the city interest demands it, the interest of the population demands it. Nonetheless, the executive committee cannot do it.

The city is zakazchik for housing construction. It knows, better than Gosplan or the republic ministries, just what needs to be built and where. And if it could decide, or at least influence the decision, then it would be possible to eliminate unnecessary, costly and even dangerous redeployment of heavy construction equipment.

Gosplan, year in and year out, actually plans for a lag in construction of schools, hospitals, childrens' institutions, trade and service facilities. Is it possible that they cannot coordinate their investment in houses and services?*

Mayor Safronov of Krasnoiarsk complained of similar problems in a speech to the Russian Supreme Soviet. The trouble, he said in 1962, was that Gosplan allocated construction funds by branches—housing, trade, health, education, municipal services—instead of by territory, that it did not balance the needs of all branches in a given district. "One must not build so that new houses lack water pipes, sewage and pedestrian underpasses," he said, "but that is often exactly what happens."[21]

Safronov asked the State Planning Commission to allocate an additional four million rubles to Krasnoiarsk in 1963 "to liquidate the

---

*Investigators taking part in the "raid" included twelve inspectors of the Party-State Control Commission, two engineers from city offices, and an Izvestiia correspondent. They noted that the soviet's lack of resources aggravated the situation. Obligated to provide contractors with equipment and materials, but lacking same, the ispolkom begged and borrowed from enterprises, and lost leverage in the process. Some Kharkov officials, tired of what the city health chief called "endless squabbling and correspondence," lapsed into irresponsibility. Acceptance commissions, said Izvestiia investigators, gave marks of "excellent" to unfinished houses, and in general, "saw what it wanted to see, instead of what was." For a frank account by the city health chief, who saw his job as "agitating" and "propagandizing" but not "threatening sanctions," see G. Torskii, "Economic Calculations and Health Services," SDT, 8 (August 1968), pp. 31-35.[20]

emergency in the sewage system and to develop transport and roads."
Gosplan chairman K. M. Gerasimov replied to Safronov and others
who, in Gerasimov's words, had "expressed themselves concerning
construction of schools, hospitals and other service facilities." "It
is expedient," he said, "to postpone consideration of additional
funds . . . until, in the course of plan fulfillment, we see how already
allocated funds are being utilized."[22] In other words the cities would
have to wait.

URBAN TRANSIT—THE POLITICS BEHIND THE RUSH HOUR

In 1966 an Izvestiia correspondent surveyed urban transit in
several province capitals: Krasnoiarsk, Omsk (821,000), Perm
(850,000), Sverdlovsk (1,026,000), Novosibirsk (1,161,000), and others.
He interviewed city officials, factory managers, architects, safety
engineers, and academic specialists on urban transit. He discovered
a crisis, analyzed its causes, and proposed a solution.[23]
    The scene at rush hour was the same in all cities: "The tram,
covered with passengers like grapes on a vine, struggles along with
great difficulty. Those who fail to hang on are strung out along the bus
stop. But other overcrowded buses pass them by."
    From this "familiar picture" flowed a multitude of social and
economic ills. Half the accidents on the Sverdlovsk city transit system
occurred when passengers lost their precarious grip and fell from
moving trams. "And how many people catch cold while wearily waiting
for the bus?" Unlike the typical Russian babushka (grandmother), the
correspondent was not concerned with stuffy noses for their own sake,
but rather with the effect of illness on production: "We are not even
talking about the more subtle effects on one's nerves and mood. Who
knows how many times doctors who certify workers 'unfit for work'
ought to cite the 'rush hour' as the cause of their illness." Statistics
showed that 2 percent of the Krasnoiarsk labor force was regularly
late for work. Experts calculated that late arrivals decreased a
worker's productivity by nearly a third, which meant that "every year,
between 150 and 160 million rubles disappear in the mud of tram and
trolley stops in the cities of the Urals and Siberia."
    How were city and industrial officials dealing with the situation?
There was a deep "pessimism" in the cities:

> Everyone is accustomed to the rush hour; they treat it like
> an inevitable evil. City officials throw up their hands; they
> say the problem has been handed down through the ages and
> is insoluble. Citizens plan their trips to work as if there
> were no problem. They allot only as much time as they

would if conditions were normal. And we really cannot
blame them for that.

Behind the pessimism was a familiar pattern. City-operated
repair facilities were inadequate. Depots and garages were built
slowly if at all. When a bus broke down in Krasnoiarsk, it had to be
shipped halfway across the country to Leningrad for capital repairs.*
One cannot imagine, wrote the correspondent, rail, air, or ocean
transport without repair bases. "But city transit, which carries an
incomparably greater number of people each day, operates without
them." Various branches were subordinate to different higher agencies:
taxis and buses to the Ministry of Auto Transport and Roads; trams
and trolleys to the Ministry of Municipal Services:

> Each ministry jealously watches each ruble it spends.
> Each tries to slough off responsibility onto the other, and
> both refer transit agencies to the local Maecenas, the
> industrial enterprises. The nominal master, the city
> ispolkom, issues only recommendations and general direc-
> tives. . . . And meanwhile, the people who actually run the
> trams and trolleys and buses go to the factories, to their
> "grandfathers and chiefs." Thus they break their necks
> over nuts and bolts and pieces of pipe.

Likewise in road construction. Bad roads abound, yet city road
repair administrations lack asphalt and construction equipment. They
must appeal to factories which have more equipment than they need:

> The factories have virtually no place to use their machin-
> ery: the parking lot, the factory grounds, the sidewalks—
> that's all. But they are rich. They can maintain all kinds

---

*Mayor Safronov, in his speech to the RSFSR Supreme Soviet,
had also complained about this. The Ministry of Municipal Services
maintained only one factory for capital repair of trams and trolleys,
and Gosplan planned production of spare parts "like a miser." In 1962
the Krasnoiarsk Tram-Trolley Administration received Gosplan's
permission to spend only 2,000 rubles on parts. Said Safronov: "It
is easier now to get a new trolley bus or tram than spare parts for
an old one. And if you add to this the fact that our city receives only
old trams—and more than ten different types of old trams—then you
see how badly Gosplan treats city transport." See RSFSR Zasedaniia
(5th call; 7th session), p. 155.

of equipment. Not so the city repair administrations.
There every kopeck is counted.

But the local Maecenas does not offer up his gold for
nothing: The city road repair men go to the factory. "Give
us a road roller," they say. "That is possible," is the
reply. "But you know the principle: 'We give you a tel-
evision; you give us a telephone.'" And so the two sides
conclude all kinds of complex deals. One can detect the
deals by looking at the road. The road is wider near one
factory; that factory was a bit richer. Near another the
road is more narrow. And next to a third, the road is a
thin film of asphalt and there is no sidewalk at all.

Nor do city agencies make up in skilled cadres what they lack
in machinery. Electric transport gets "hurriedly retrained railroad
men, electricians, sanitation men and God knows who else." The head
of the Krasnoiarsk Tram-Trolley Administration (himself an ex-
railroader) recalled how he and his men gazed upon a new trolley "as
if it were some kind of bewitching box." Sverdlovsk's personnel
training chief, lacking sample vehicles, instructs his men "on our fin-
gers and with maps and posters."

Izvestiia could find no silver lining in the cloud of transit
exhaust. Cities were growing and rush hours were getting worse. "It
would be incorrect to assert that nothing at all is being done," the
reporter noted glumly. "In a few places they are trying to decrease
dependence on enterprises. They are building little pavilions at bus
stops to protect passengers from wind and rain." More important,
long-range transportation plans have been devised for many cities.
But some blueprints "do not take the specific features of cities into
account," and others are useless since cities lack urban plans regulating future development.*

Despite their legitimate grievances, city officials must also
share the blame. They did not make most efficient use of admittedly
insufficient resources. They "break their backs trying to solve simple
problems," said Izvestiia. Krasnoiarsk spent two years determining
how to raze a house blocking the approach to a new bridge. Sverdlovsk
took too long to open a new transit dispatcher's office; officials used

---

*The Izvestiia correspondent cites examples: "The Krasnoiarsk
transit plan is destined to fail since . . . no one knows in what direction
the city will grow. Likewise, Sverdlovsk, Novosibirsk and Perm do
not know their future fate. Only a few cities in the RSFSR have general plans as well as transit plans."

overloaded telephone lines while new radio-communications equipment gathered dust in a warehouse.

Action to end the cities' transit crisis must come, Izvestiia said, on several fronts:

1. All branches of transit should be unified in enlarged municipal transportation administrations.

2. The new administrations must be equipped with repair and maintenance bases. Funds and equipment for road construction, now allocated to factories, must be transferred to cities. Personnel—drivers, conductors, mechanics—must be better paid and trained in programs that include study of foreign transit systems.

3. The central government must immediately spend 100 million rubles to liquidate "the basic transportation mess" in the large cities of the Urals and Siberia alone. The sum was large, but Gosplan must remember the 150-million-ruble cost of employee lateness; it must stop "economizing on the crumbs and losing the heaps."*

THEME AND VARIATIONS: WHO IS TO BLAME?

Inadequate central subsidies, self-interested action by non-city agencies, soviets' own incompetence—the mix varies from city to city.

Ineptitude without mitigating circumstances—this was the charge levelled against Tomsk (339,000), by a Sovety deputatov correspondent who often defends soviets from similar attacks by enterprises. The

---

*In January 1968 the USSR Council of Ministers issued a decree, "On Measures for Improving Urban Passenger Transit Service." It proposed unification of transit services in enlarged city agencies, construction of repair depots and other backup facilities, new training programs and transit plans for all cities with populations greater than 250,000. The decree is translated in CDSP, XX, No. 4 (1968) p. 25. For a survey of culture similar to Izvestiia's study of transit, see M. Sokol'skii, "Against Departmental Divisions," SDT, 9 (September 1966), pp. 29-34. Cities examined include province centers (Omsk, Rostov on Don, 789,000; Karaganda, 522,000); one republic capital (Alma Ata, 730,000); and others, including Temirtau (founded 1945; 167,000), Podolsk (founded 1781; 169,000), and Orekhovo-Zuevo (founded 1917; 120,000). Municipal cultural administrators depended on enterprises, particularly in new and small cities. "Managers . . . are the ones who lay out money for culture," said a Temirtau official, "So we cannot very well tell them what to do." "Rarely," concludes the report, "do workers in cultural organs give battle against obstinate managers."

trouble in Tomsk, wrote I. Serikov, was "not in the enterprises, but
in the style and work of the executive committee," which did not spend
funds allotted to it and ended up returning them to the province soviet
at the end of the year.[24]

Why were the funds not spent? Due to lack of materials to spend
them on? In Arkhangelsk (343,000), said Sovety deputatov, city hall's
credo was: "If I want to do it I will; if not I won't."[25] But city leaders
blamed superiors for not supplying funds and materials required by
a far northern city. In violation of established norms, factories built
new houses of wood. No doubt they lacked other building materials.
For the city to forbid such construction would aggravate the housing
shortage, which only the enterprises were wealthy enough to remedy.[26]

Millions of square meters of housing have been erected in the
last ten years in Penza (374,000), reported Pravda in 1969. "But can
one say it has become a handsome and modern city, a comfortable
city for its residents? Can one point out any finished section of
construction, and say proudly that the whole city will soon look like
it? Unfortunately, no."[27] City planners had issued detailed guidelines, which both industry and the mayor ignored. Enterprises developed industrial districts as they saw fit, an approach that "conflicts
with the very essence of the planned socialist economy." The city
built an apartment complex that was enclosed on all sides by railroad
tracks and a highway, and erected another "on a slope specified in the
plan as an active landslide zone." These were "gross violations of
municipal building norms," but "not a single meeting of the Penza
Executive Committeee has examined implementation of the plan."

Dnepropetrovsk (755,000) officials operated, wrote correspondent
Serikov, according to a standard bureaucratic motto: "We take on
just enough so that they will not condemn us, but not enough so that
our heads will hurt from overwork."[28] The mayor told a different
story.[29] City planners, he said, had assumed an annual population
increase of 10,000 to 12,000, reaching a total of 1,100,000 between
1985 and 1990. Now (1969) it appeared that the one-million mark would
be reached in 1973 instead. Why? Because industrial expansion,
outdistancing housing and service construction, had "spurted sharply
in a short period of time." The mayor insisted that he had tried to
restrain the enterprises, but that the latter "showed their cards" only
at the last minute. The USSR Ministry of Ferrous Metallurgy opened
a plant employing 4,000 workers but allotted no funds for housing,
schools, or stores. "They pin their hopes on the city soviet," said
the mayor, "but it is absolutely impossible for us to provide the
missing facilities." What Dnepropetrovsk needed, he said, was more
help from "our principal guardian, the Ministry of Municipal Services,"
plus an undertaking by industry to spend more on nonindustrial
projects. Remarking that the soviet's burden was "a rather heavy one,"

the mayor insisted that he not be misunderstood. "I do not advocate lightening or removing the burden. Not at all."

Consider Gorky (1,170,000) in 1968. "Routine governmental operations," wrote the mayor, "required three times as much money as is allocated, to say nothing of future development. . . ."30 The city had appealed to enterprises but they granted aid like "handouts from a rich relative," complete with "conditions that are not always acceptable to the city." Some industrial executives had to be "beaten down" before they would contribute, as in the case of the Gorky Railroad, which was forbidden to connect a newly opened apartment building to the city utilities. Nor could factory managers be blamed, since their superiors "give preference to industrial facilities, relegating housing and services to second rank." What was needed, wrote the mayor, were regular deductions from enterprise profits and increased availability of enterprise funds.

Consider Zaporozhe (658,000) in 1962. Non-city agencies owned 88 percent of public housing; nine different enterprises operated private water and sewage systems. Factory managers waxed eloquent on their willingness to transfer such facilities to the city. Said the director of Zaporozhe Steel: "All our vast and complex service facilities are really of little value to us. Production is our main interest. We cannot devote sufficient attention to the service sector. And even if the present system were useful to us, it is bad for the general state interest and for welfare of the city as a whole."

The head of Dnepro Gas agreed that transfer was "long overdue." Another director admitted that "as manager I find it convenient to have my own services, but as citizen I see that this makes for an abnormal situation." Only one said he needed facilities to attract employees, and he was assured that a deal would be worked out that would not hinder his recruitment.31

Despite the apparent harmony, though, transfer was delayed. City officials said they would need 300 of the 900 men presently on factory service staffs. The enterprises said they could not afford to lose men, and even pressure from the city Party authorities could not budge them. Complaining to Sovety deputatov was the city soviet's next move. The editors responded by demanding action from the Zaporozhe Province Soviet and the Ukrainian Council of Ministers.

Why did managers object? Did they want to shift service personnel to production jobs? Or was their reluctance a tactic designed to thwart transfer of nonindustrial facilities? Whatever their motive, their approach was classic—invoking ambiguous central instructions (which did not mention personnel) to protect their interests, using the letter of the law to dodge its spirit.

The same ploy was used in Novosibirsk, where the soviet's superiors, for their own reasons, sided with industry. In 1955, 155

non-soviet enterprises were zakazchiki in Novosibirsk. By 1958 the
soviet, with the help of the city Party committee, had assumed
zakazchik powers itself.[32] Next, the city sought transfer of housing
and service facilities. Its arguments seemed persuasive: municipal
housing was better maintained and more profitable. The regional
economic council and the Ministry of Finance approved the change.
But the former refused to transfer men to the city, and the latter,
citing its hallowed Marxist mandate to reduce white collar staffs,
"asked the soviet not to insist on an increase." Then, wrote the mayor,

> there began financial casuistry beyond enduring. It turns
> out the enterprise may pay numberless functionaries out of
> the central fund allotted to them. That's fine. But to move
> a few of those men to the borough housing office is impos-
> sible. No one wants to understand that such a move would
> save money needed for other work. Imagine a merger of
> two enterprises. No one would object to merging staffs of
> economists, engineers, etc. Why then is the soviet, after
> taking over enterprise housing, prohibited from taking a few
> men from the hundreds who used to work for the factories?
>   But instead we have an endless argument with the
> deputy minister of finance. We proved to him that it's
> irrational to spend so much on splintered agency staffs.
> "We see that ourselves," said the deputy minister.
> "But where can we get the authority to increase your
> staff? No, no. We are supposed to cut down city
> bureaucracies. So we had better let things stay the
> way they are. . . ."[33]

The Novosibirsk chairman was aware of charges of sloth levelled
against other soviets. He rejected in advance any innuendoes against
his: "Can it be said that we do not want to take on added responsibility?
No, it cannot. We do want it. We are ready. But to function effectively we must have what Moscow and Leningrad have—machinery,
trained cadres, repair bases, new and bigger housing offices. . . ."

Leaders of new and small cities envy those of province capitals, just as leaders of province capitals envy those of Moscow and Leningrad. In province centers, apparent advantages bring liabilities: owning housing and services, but lacking resources, soviets must depend on enterprises; as zakazchiki, executive committees depend on superiors whose instructions inhibit local initiative. But Moscow and Leningrad authorities appear equipped, by virtue of their position in the governmental hierarchy, to turn greater advantages into extensive power and influence. Moscow (1970 population: 7,061,000) and Leningrad (3,950,000) report directly to republic agencies, without going through province soviets. (Moscow leaders have the further advantage of dealing with all-union agencies on the spot.) The Moscow City Soviet bargained with the Moscow City Regional Economic Council on a one-to-one basis; Leningrad, less fortunate, had to cope with a council that encompassed Leningrad, Novgorod, and Pskov provinces as well as the city. If any city leaders have sufficient personal authority and prestige to confront industrial ministers (who also live in the Soviet capital), Moscow and Leningrad officials are the ones; mayors are important personages, and city Party leaders are among the most influential in the ruling elite.

At first glance the record appears to bear out these expectations. In 1956 the Leningrad soviet operated 73.3 percent of Leningrad housing, while in Moscow the soviet owned 57 percent. By 1965 the Leningrad share of housing space was 87 percent (virtually all except university housing, cooperatives, and private homes), and in both cities, according to the Institute of State and Law, "the major share of services was in the hands of local soviets."[1] "In general, the enterprises do not make trouble for us," said the chairman of a Moscow borough soviet, who also headed a city soviet standing committee. "We build the roads, the schools and the houses so they do not want to offend us."[2]

The borough chairman said that city and non-city authorities preferred to resolve controversial questions quietly because each realized the value of working together. Cattell detected a similar pattern in Leningrad. But when persuasion fails, these mayors were not afraid to enforce their ordinances. The Moscow Executive Committee's bulletin chronicles its actions: it rebukes enterprises for not keeping premises clean and threatens fines; it pressures them to prepare housing for winter; it takes away land granted to a factory when construction does not proceed as planned. While smaller cities complain in vain about polluters of air and water, Moscow and Leningrad act vigorously. Moscow "demands" that the regional economic council prepare pollution control plans including one in its giant Likhachev Auto Factory, and "warns" factory directors that they will be held personally responsible for fulfilling these plans. Moscow announces a victory: the council has agreed that all new factories will be equipped with pollution-control devices.[3] Similarly, in Leningrad, soviet authorities publicly pressured guilty enterprises until they installed anti-pollution systems.[4]

But if successes are documented, so are some familiar problems. In 1962 a Moscow official named A. M. Pegov told the RSFSR Supreme Soviet that municipal services—water supply, sewage, roads—were not keeping pace with the industrial and population growth. In March 1966 a borough chairman complained that new residential districts were being built in a haphazard way; houses were on schedule but stores and services were delayed. In 1963 Z. Kruglova, a Leningrad Party secretary, reported that "the service sphere, despite many successes, remains the least successful branch of our economy."[5]

Why these problems? Official Moscow and Leningrad bulletins allot a large measure of blame to the city governments themselves. Cattell estimates that 20 percent of the resolutions published in Leningrad in 1961, "denounced the shortcomings of city departments. . . ."[6] Moscow bulletins of the 1960s record a variety of problems: plans unfulfilled; officials ineffective, insensitive, or simply stupid; a crippling lack of trained cadres, especially in the service sector. More than 43 percent of those in "engineering-technical" posts lack specialized education, and in one borough the figure is as high as 70 percent; a borough services administration fired more than 80 men or 36.1 percent of its "leading technical workers" in two years; more than 13,000 workers in various borough departments and enterprises were fired in 1964 and 1965. The bulletins plead for self-improvement. If only officials in charge of cadre training would "show more initiative," and "follow Party recruitment principles more faithfully," and "be more demanding of their subordinates," then the situation could be drastically improved.[7]

But the city governments' shortcomings are only part of the
story. In Moscow and Leningrad, soviets also have grievances against
non-city agencies and their own superiors. The agencies (industrial
and other) expand operations so rapidly that city-managed services
cannot keep pace; and superiors, who could help close the gap, do not.
The agencies try to delay transfer of zakazchik powers; then higher
planning authorities prevent the soviets from using those powers
effectively. In addition to fighting for housing and services, and for
zakazchik powers, Moscow and Leningrad lead other cities in two
more campaigns—to limit industrial expansion, and for a reduction
in central controls over city soviet spending.

INDUSTRY NOT WANTED

Compare Moscow with Riga, capital of the Latvian Republic.
"Industry is thousands of people," declared Latvia's Planning Commission chairman in 1966; "thousands of citizens who need services."
But industrial agencies "do not consider that a new factory means
building water pipes, sewage systems, new stores, cultural centers
and other enterprises. . . ." Riga, said the chairman, "has clearly
expanded past its optimal dimension," creating a serious shortage
of services. Riga's remedy had been to post a certain-industries-
not-wanted sign. It welcomed "modern enterprises of advanced
technology which can service already existing plants," but considered
that "construction of mammoth new enterprises is not expedient."
How had the industrial agencies reacted? As reported in Izvestiia:

> Some comrades do not understand a rather simple fact—
> that a huge industrial center hides the effect of an in-
> dividual enterprise on all-city expenditures. In a small
> city or a settlement, the cost of developing the city ser-
> vices is clear, and it certainly increases the cost of
> building the enterprise. This is the optical illusion
> which scares ministries away from the periphery and
> forces them to grasp with both hands for the huge urban
> center.[8]

To read the Moscow Bulletin, one would think its executive
committee, in contrast to Riga's, had been able to control the pace
of industrial expansion. It allots land for new enterprises and
reconstruction of old ones only after extensive consideration. It
oversees project planning and drafting of blueprints. It cancels land
allotments when ministries fail to carry out plans the city has
approved.[9]

Yet this activity is deceiving. For if the soviet can influence details, it cannot affect the basic decision of whether or not to build. So said Moscow official Pegov to the Russian Supreme Soviet in December 1962. Industrial construction, he explained, constituted 50 percent of the total volume of capital investment in Moscow, but "the Moscow Executive Committee has no control over it." The ispolkom could not "influence the planning of non-soviet capital investments or evaluate the expediency of this construction." The city could not prevent the agencies from "ignoring such all-city needs as electricity, water supply, sewage and roads . . . contributing to the backwardness of several branches of the city economy."

Moscow's chief architect had complained at the 1960 city planning conference that "We still experience great pressure from state committees, ministries and other agencies in charge of the economy— all trying, by any and all means to build in Moscow."[10] Moscow's answer, described by Pegov in 1962, was to propose a new long-range plan that could ensure "balanced growth of all sectors of the city economy" by regulating the amount of capital construction and the size of the labor force. The plan would be linked "with an extension of the rights of the Moscow Executive Committee in the planning and execution of capital investment . . . and would permit the soviet not only to know about, but also to influence everything done in the city by non-soviet agencies; it would enable the ispolkom to coordinate agency planning with the general development of the city and its economy."[11]

As Pegov spoke, Moscow planners were completing "Technical-Economic Bases (TEB) for a General Plan for the Development of Moscow until 1980." Shortly after the session, the soviet and the Moscow Party Committee jointly submitted the TEB to the USSR government for approval.

The TEB stated clearly the soviet's intention to limit the growth of Moscow by forbidding "construction of new or expansion of existing industrial enterprises, scientific-research and drafting institutes, construction bureaus, experimental bases, higher educational institutions—all with the exception of such enterprises and objects which directly serve the population and meet the needs of housing and civil construction."[12]

The TEB called for an increase in production and in the quality of goods produced, but without an increase in the labor force. It counted on a rise in labor productivity fueled by new technology and automation. Moscow would welcome "specialized industry" (precision machine-building, and electronics plants), as well as factories manufacturing consumer goods of particularly high quality. Of existing plants, certain small factories would either be eliminated or combined, and plants creating fire and health hazards would be ousted from

Moscow, as would those using excessive water, electricity, and fuel, and those scientific and educational institutions without special reasons for being in the capital. ("Do we really need seven higher institutions studying the seas and oceans?" asked Moscow Mayor V. F. Promyslov in 1967. "Wouldn't it be better to move them a bit closer to the seashore?")[13] The population would be limited to somewhere between 6.6 and 6.8 million. Free at last of relentless population pressure, the city would launch a massive program to end the service lag, "to guarantee rational use of the city's territory for construction of housing, and municipal, cultural and consumers' services. . . ."*

In 1963, Moscow authorities looked forward to early approval of the TEB. Mayor Promyslov** noted in December that the USSR Council of Ministers and CPSU Central Committee had issued a joint resolution reaffirming the goal of limiting the expansion of cities.[15] At the suggestion of the central committee, Moscow had asked the State Construction Committee to reconsider its earlier approval of new industrial construction in Moscow, valued at 250 million rubles. A Moscow spokesman promised that in 1964 the city would draft a complete plan based on the TEB. "We hope," he said, "that state committees, ministries and other agencies will take an active role in implementing the plan."[16]

But approval of the TEB did not come as easily as Moscow hoped. Simple bureaucratic inertia? Or active resistance from those who found the plan inconvenient? Whatever the reason, the delay was so frustrating that Moscow Party chief N. G. Egorychev***

---

*To ensure compliance, the ispolkom and its architecture-planning administration were to have a voice in day-to-day planning. They would "examine" ministries' plans for Moscow enterprises and "would help define basic indicators and directions of growth . . . through 1980."[14]

**Promyslov became chairman in 1963, and a member of the CPSU Central Committee in 1966. Before that he held the following posts: RSFSR Minister of Construction (1963); chairman, RSFSR Gosstroi (1959-63); first deputy chairman, Moscow Executive Committee (1955-59); secretary, Moscow City Party Committee (1954-55); USSR Deputy Minister of Higher Education (1951-53); and deputy chairman for construction, Moscow Executive Committee (1949-51, 1953-54).

***Before becoming first secretary in 1962 (and a member of the Central Committee in 1961), Egorychev held the following posts: second secretary, Moscow (1961-62); Central Committee instructor (1960-61); second, then first, secretary, Bauman Borough Party Committee (1954-60). Regarded by Western sovietologists as a rising

felt compelled to complain publicly, to the USSR Supreme Soviet in
1964:

> Many great scholars, architects, economists, engineers
> and the Moscow public itself helped to prepare the
> Technical-Economic Bases of the General Plan. Yet
> in almost two years, the USSR State Planning and State
> Construction Committees have not managed to finish
> discussing it. We ask Gosplan and Gosstroi to present
> their conclusions to the government as soon as possible
> for it is difficult to build a great city such as Moscow
> without a long-range plan.

Egorychev's speech and his cosponsorship of the TEB indicated
the importance Party authorities attached to the case. Nonetheless
the first secretary strove to avoid complete identification with the
soviet's views. He did not endorse Promyslov's campaign (see below)
to liberate municipal construction from excessive planning commission
tutelage, and he rejected the role of special pleader for the city
interest. "We would not want you to think," said Egorychev," that Moscow
is a city which demands much from the state and gives little. That
would be a mistaken opinion."[17]
In December 1965, with the TEB still not approved, Promyslov
protested again to the Supreme Soviet:

> We must forcefully restrain the ambitions of many eco-
> nomic organizations, state committees, and ministries
> trying to create and expand . . . enterprises in Moscow.
> For despite everything, in the last six years the number
> of people working only in scientific-research, construction
> and similar organizations has grown by 256,000.
>   We consider it incorrect that these organizations
> are concentrated in such great numbers in Moscow when,
> without any harm to their work, they might be located
> in other regions of the country.
>   We think that USSR Gosplan, together with the
> Moscow Executive Committee and interested ministries
> and state committees, ought to confront this matter, which
> is so important to Muscovites, and settle it.[18]

---

star, Egorychev was replaced in 1967 by V. Grishin, member of the
Central Committee (since 1952) and Politburo (candidate-member
since 1961), who served as chairman of All-Union Trade Union
Council (1956-67) and second secretary, Moscow (1952-56).

To speed this settlement and to help enforce it, Promyslov proposed creation of a new department in the State Planning Commission, one that would coordinate city plans with those of ministries and agencies. No doubt he had in mind the fact that, as economist A. Birman has written, "how Gosplan disposes of a social product of a certain size . . . depends to a considerable degree . . . on the correlation of forces among Gosplan's individual departments."[19]

Even as Promyslov spoke, however, the stalemate over TEB was apparently breaking up. On August 24, 1965 the USSR Council of Ministers declared once again that it "would not permit excessive concentration of industrial enterprises in large cities. . . ." On February 12, 1966 an RSFSR decree gave Moscow authority "to examine plans of USSR and RSFSR ministries and agencies concerning the location and development of new industry and . . . the reconstruction and expansion of existing enterprises." In March 1966 the Twenty-Third Party Congress endorsed the principle of limiting big-city growth. On September 6, 1966 the USSR Council of Ministers finally approved the TEB—"in general form," said the Moscow Soviet's announcement.[20]

On October 4, 1966 the Moscow City Soviet met to celebrate the turning point. Letting bygones be bygones, Promyslov expressed "deep gratitude to the Central Committee and the Soviet government for the vast attention with which they examined the Technical-Economic Bases."[21] He pledged to seek the cooperation of ministries and agencies in drafting the plan itself. But those with whom he sought cooperation were neither so grateful nor as sanguine as he. Only the tip of the opposition iceberg broke through the session's typically placid surface. No representative of industry complained, but Academician N. M. Emmanuel expressed the discontent of the USSR Academy of Sciences. His speech was remarkably glum for such an occasion. He said facilities for scientific research in Moscow were not overdeveloped, as the city contended, but rather underdeveloped. He suggested that "the authors of the general plan should visit Kiev to see what beautiful modern facilities are constructed there for the Ukrainian Academy of Science," and remarked that "similarly comforting pictures might be seen in capitals of other union republics." Moscow's plan would force the academy outside the city, where it would have to build not only laboratories but whole cities, including "municipal and other services, schools, stores, hospitals, etc." If only it could build "a few particularly important institutes in Moscow, without any limitations or obstacles, then the Academy would have more to spend" on research. The present five-year plan envisaged construction in Moscow of three new institutes (Mathematics, Geography, and Mathematical Economics), as well as buildings for the Academy's publishing house, Nauka, and its presidium. "But," concluded

Emmanuel, "this is too little. It would be desirable if the Moscow City Soviet would devote a special session to the creation in Moscow of modern first-class scientific institutions."[22]

Was industry's silence at the session a sign of strength? If bans had been bypassed before, why not in the future? I. T. Novikov, deputy chairman of the USSR Council of Ministers and chairman of USSR Gosstroi, hinted as much when he warned that Moscow would face continuing opposition from industrial agencies, and that "some organizations" were already "finding loopholes" and continuing to build in Moscow.*

But even if industrial expansion were slowed, would municipal resources suffice? The city construction trust, said its deputy director, lacked funds and trained personnel, and "could not cope either with the volume or new character of construction."[24] He pleaded for more assistance from higher up. But if the city's superiors had supported the soviet—in words, at least**—in its campaign to halt expansion of Moscow, they were not so generous with funds or their own prerogatives. Like province center authorities, Moscow officials had to lobby for more aid and for the freedom to use hard-earned zakazchik powers.

THE IMPORTANCE OF BEING ZAKAZCHIK

For Moscow, as for other cities, the July 31, 1957 decree on zakazchik rights did not have an immediate effect. The year 1958 brought no changes. In June 1959, Promyslov, then deputy mayor, protested to a central committee plenum called to discuss

---

*Two months later a Leningrad spokesman indicated that his city shared Moscow's problems and envied its solution. Said G. V. Romanov, secretary of the Leningrad Province Party Committee and former City Party secretary: "We hold that reconstruction and re-equipment of enterprises without increasing the size of the payroll must become the chief trend . . . in Leningrad enterprises as well as in those Comrade Promyslov discussed." He called for new USSR Gosplan departments "for such cities as Moscow, Leningrad and others;" the existing territorial planning departments of RSFSR Gosplan had, he said, "no influence over a number of all-union ministries." See speech to USSR Supreme Soviet, in Izvestiia, December 17, 1966, pp. 3-4.[23]

**The qualification, "in words, at least," seems necessary in view of the fact that despite all the decrees and exhortations, the agencies managed to keep expanding in Moscow and other large cities.

implementation of recent decisions "accelerating technical progress in industry and construction." On behalf of other cities besides Moscow, he complained that the transfer of zakazchik authority had begun only in 1959. Had certain ministries and state committees convinced the government to go back on its promise? On May 30, 1958 another USSR decree had designated a series of agencies that could continue to act as zakazchik, and the RSFSR government had offered similar dispensation to 25 more agencies. This meant, said Promyslov, that "besides the Moscow City Soviet there are nearly 50 ministries and agencies in Moscow which invest in construction themselves and distribute funds to other enterprises which also act as zakazchiki." The result was the same in the capital as in other cities: uncoordinated construction, residential districts without stores and services, high costs, and project completion dates that were rarely met. "To eliminate these shortcomings," said Promyslov, "the July 31, 1957 decree . . . must be fully implemented beginning in 1960. All planned capital investments in housing and service construction must be allocated directly to the Moscow City Executive Committee."[25]

When did Moscow receive zakazchik rights? In 1960, said one source.[26] But apparently later years brought further dispensations, for it was only in 1967 that a city spokesman could write: "Beginning this year all centralized capital investments will be allocated to the Moscow City Soviet . . . whereas at one time there were more than 500 zakazchiki."[27]

But even before 1967, Moscow and Leningrad, like province centers, had discovered that rigid central controls prevented effective use of centrally allocated resources. Leningrad officials raised the issue at the 1960 all-union conference on city planning and at the USSR Supreme Soviet session in 1960. Khrushchev himself appeared to take notice of the cities' complaints at the central committee plenum of November 1962; but when no basic change followed, spokesmen for Moscow, Leningrad, and Kiev (1,632,000) raised the issue again at the USSR Supreme Soviet session in December 1962.[28] The campaign reached a crescendo at a similar session in December 1964. V. I. Drozdenko,* first secretary of the Kiev Province Party Committee summed up the cities' case:

---

*Drozdenko became first secretary in 1960. After 1962 he became: first secretary, Kiev Province (industrial) committee (1962-64); first secretary, Kiev Province (1964-66); secretary of the Ukrainian Central Committee and member of its presidium, and candidate member of the CPSU Central Committee (in 1966).

The present system of planning capital investments in the
city economy by branches prevents coordinated construction of cities. At present, the procedure is as follows:
first they allot funds for housing construction, then for
cultural and service projects, for hospitals, schools,
and stores. But these are not coordinated. This creates
a situation in which houses are finished on schedule, but
service projects are not built for years, meaning great
inconvenience for the population.

Much has been said about this at sessions of the
Supreme Soviet. We have heard speeches of deputies
from Moscow, Leningrad, and various cities in the Urals
and along the Volga. But the planning system remains
the same. It must be changed.[29]

Moscow's chief architect M. V. Posokhin proposed changes.
"Gosplan," he said, "must establish a general sum of capital investment for each residential district. That sum must include construction of houses, public buildings and services so that each district
becomes the focus of drafting, planning, financing, construction and
operation." Equally important, city executive committees should be
authorized to redistribute funds among the various branches in each
district.[30]

"The old method of planning should have been altered long ago,"
said Posokhin, a sentiment shared by G. I. Popov, Leningrad first
secretary.* In a particularly caustic passage, Popov reminded the
government that for several years deputies had "unceasingly" pressed
for the new planning system:

The usefulness of the suggestion is so obvious that no
one has voiced objection. However, the problem has not
been settled up to the present time. And meanwhile,
planning of investment in city construction continues according to branches with all the inevitable negative consequences.

There arises, therefore, some justified bewilder-
ment. If the deputies have been introducing an unaccept-
able suggestion all these years, then one would think that
it would have been possible to explain their error. If, on

---

*Popov became first secretary in 1960, and a member of the
CPSU Central Committee in 1964. Before that he was second
secretary, Leningrad Province (1957-60), and first secretary of
the Vyborg city Party committee (1956-57).

the other hand, the proposal merits approval, then it
should have been examined and acted upon. However,
neither one course nor the other has been followed.[31]

But the cities did not achieve satisfaction in 1965 or in 1966.
In December 1965 Mayor Promyslov returned to the Supreme Soviet
rostrum to urge again the change he and his colleagues had requested
so many times before.[32] Shortly thereafter the Moscow Executive
Committee formally submitted specific programs to Gosplan, Gosstroi,
and the USSR Ministry of Finance. But in December 1966, when
Promyslov addressed the parliament again, he complained that "they
have by no means decided these questions. . . ."[33]

Why did central authorities respond so slowly? Were ministries
in charge of each branch protecting their right to dominate city
departments subordinate to them? Were the planning commission's
branch departments repulsing a threat to their power? Whatever
the reason, city leaders saw their superiors' reluctance as part of
a pattern of insensitivity.

To the chairman of Novosibirsk, Moscow and Leningrad may
seem fortunate. But leaders of the two giants are not satisfied. A
Leningrad spokesman told the Supreme Soviet that, while central
authorities planned for a 3.7-percent rate of growth for housing,
they projected only a 3-percent increase for services—although
these already lagged.[34] Moscow's Pegov complained that, despite
the lag, investment in service construction, taken as a percentage of
state investment in housing, dropped from 47 percent in 1957 to 38.7
percent in 1962.[35]

How does the central government respond to these complaints?
Novikov, who was later to become chairman of the State Construction
Committee, took note of them at the October 1966 session of the
Moscow City Soviet. Reminding Moscow of its favored position, he
said it could not expect unlimited aid. In response to the Moscow
construction administrator's pleas for more assistance, Novikov
insisted that "in comparison with . . . other cities in our country,
Moscow leads the way. . . ."[36]

11

WHO GOVERNS?

Chervonograd, to return to the small Ukrainian city mentioned in the Preface, is not unique or even extreme. In a great many Soviet cities urban development has been uneven, housing and services have lagged behind industrial development, non-city agencies have dominated city soviets, and municipal governments have been unable or unwilling to govern.

WHY?

Why? In part the urban syndrome reflects the priorities of the central leadership. Those Americans who are enamored of planning—including some who look admiringly at Soviet cities—should remember that the planners' values make a difference. To the Soviet leaders, to the military-heavy industrial complex for which they so often seem to speak, industrialization has been sacred above almost everything.[1] Industrialization has set the pace and shaped the quality of urbanization. Industries have developed previously backward areas, revitalized stagnant towns, and sparked spectacular growth of larger centers— but at a high cost in shortages, dislocations, and in some cities a situation little short of chaos.*

---

*If industrialization, which brought about the massive shift in the labor force from agriculture to manufacturing, is the basic motor of urbanization, there are of course other concurrent and in part autonomous causes; among them are overall population growth and the lure of the urban way of life. Parallels with turn-of-the-century America are particularly striking: cities growing with great rapidity,

To be sure, there have been notable achievements. While
trailing U.S. cities in the supply of consumer services and certain
municipal services as well, Soviet cities are generally better supplied
with inexpensive public transportation, with medical clinics, and with
such recreational and educational facilities as parks and child-care
centers. Between 1956 and 1970 more housing was erected in the
USSR than in any other country in the world, whether one measures
in absolute figures or per capita ones.[2] Nonetheless Soviet municipal
governments have lacked needed resources because central authorities,
concentrating their efforts on industry, have not provided sufficient
assistance. Such neglect is doubly damaging: it shortchanges city-run
services directly, and it forces the city to beg aid from industrial
enterprises, which, in return, may demand the right to continue the
practices that aggravate urban ills in the first place. Answerable for
housing and services, mayors preside over shortage; responsible for
the law, soviets countenance its violation; guardian of the city interest,
the ispolkom fails at city planning. Municipal personnel are often
ill-trained, ill-equipped, and ill-paid; understandably city leaders can
become discouraged. But municipal incompetence, whatever its cause,
impedes reform. Cities may seek more authority and more funds,
but non-city agencies and higher authorities, reluctant anyway to yield
scarce resources, are even more chary of giving them to ineffective
municipal administrations.*
      The effect on the quality of city life is clear. But shortages and
dislocations also harm industry itself. City officials have pointed this
out, as has the eminent Soviet economist L. Kantorovich:

      . . . much in everyday services still fails to meet the
      Soviet people's increased demands. The organization,

---

municipal governments powerless to control the pace and direction of
industrial expansion. See Mel Scott, American City Planning Since
1890 (Berkeley: University of California Press, 1969).
      *President Nixon offered revenue-sharing as his answer to a
somewhat similar American vicious circle. He recognized, in his
1971 State of the Union address, that state and local governments are
"so weak they approach impotence." His prescription was to give them
"a larger share of the nation's responsibilities," and a share of federal
revenues (in "new and unrestricted funds" rather than "narrow purpose
aid programs"), "so that they can meet those responsibilities." The
same words serve admirably as a summary of what many Soviet city
leaders sought in the post-1957 era. See The New York Times,
January 23, 1971, p. 12.

equipment, cadres and labor productivity of this branch
lag substantially behind the production branches. . . .
Yet . . . the organization of everyday services is important for production. A person's diligence, frame of
mind, and interest in productive labor depend on how he
travelled to and from work, on how he spent his lunch
break and the time after work. The conveniences of everyday life (public cafeterias, children's institutions) substantially influence labor resources and the stability of
cadres.[3]

Economic planners and managers may accept this argument in
principle, but in practice they resist change. Imperatives of the
command economy explain their behavior: intense pressure to produce demands single-minded concentration on short-term goals;
scarcity encourages competition for and hoarding of resources.
Ironically, though, efforts to reform the command economy do not
necessarily improve the urban situation, and they may in fact make it
worse. Managers are urged to care more about the quality of goods,
but what about the quality of city life? The system now rewards them
for sales and profits instead of gross output, but not for good works.
Factories are encouraged to look after their own welfare, but what
about the general urban welfare?

For those who view "innovative technocrats" as the wave of the
Soviet future, this picture should be unsettling. Both city planners
and factory managers are technocrats; so too are leading urban
Party officials, many of whom are former managers.[4] The question
then is not who is winning a conflict between Party and technocrats,
but rather which technocrats control the ruling Party—except that it
is another lesson of this study that the image of centralized Party
rule is itself in need of some revision.

If central planners' preferences were the full answer, if the
Party were as decisive as it is supposed to be in the hierarchical
system, then change should have come more easily. After all, the
regime has been paying more attention recently to urban problems;
the Party has given balanced urban development a somewhat higher
priority than previously. But there are other forces at work. The
legacy of an earlier era—bureaucratic arrangements, institutional
relationships, constellations of forces—lives on to plague the new.
The old framework was not designed and is not suited to achieving
new goals; yet it resists change. The central leadership cannot
reform that framework without the kind of massive assault that, for
a variety of reasons, it has hesitated to undertake.

WHO GOVERNS?

All this complicates the attempt to answer the traditional
question of politics—who governs? This is, however, as it should be,
since efforts to discover who governs American communities have
unearthed enough complications to fuel an extended scholarly debate,
to produce what one observer has described as "a dialectical pattern
in which a series of assertions is advanced and then attacked,"
followed by "a third phase which consists of an attempt to salvage the
first set of assertions."5

The first set of assertions concerning American community
power was advanced by such sociologists as C. Wright Mills and
Floyd Hunter. They found communities dominated by socioeconomic
elites—by social and economic "notables," as Robert Dahl, a critic of
Mills and Hunter, was later to call them. The "elitist view" of
community power was attacked by pluralist critics (among them Dahl,
Nelson Polsby, and others), who found power to be dispersed among
a variety of individuals and groups. Third to answer have been
"neo-elitists" who point not to an identifiable organized elite
manipulating community power but to the built-in limits of American
pluralism, to a hidden "mobilization of bias" that produces a "false
consensus" in support of a fundamentally unjust political-economic
system.6

I shall say more about the American debate in a broader context below. For the moment, the argument is this: although the
Western study of Soviet cities has not kept pace with American
community power studies (in the sense that there has been no systematic
attempt to answer the question of who governs, and certainly no
dialectical pattern of disagreement), there does exist what one could
call an "elitist" view of Soviet community power. In the American
context, the elitist view has been a decidedly non-Establishment
approach, at least among political scientists. But among analysts of
Soviet politics, it has been, as I have indicated, the accepted orthodoxy.
The Soviet elite in question is of course the Party, or, to be more
precise (which not all elite analysts always are), the Party apparat.
But with all due respect for the Party, as well as for such analysts,
this book has shown that the Party apparat's power has been
exaggerated, and that what is needed for the analysis of Soviet politics
is a more pluralist approach.

As in the case of the American community power debate, the
observer's choice of actors and issues is most important. If one
focuses, as some have done, on the municipal administration
proper—which is to say the city soviet and its subordinate departments
and enterprises—it is indeed the case that urban Party and higher-level

government authorities virtually dominate the city government.* But
they do not dominate urban governance viewed as a political process
in which non-city industrial agencies play an important part. On
nonindustrial issues, city soviet officials necessarily exert influence
by virtue of their position as responsible authorities "on the ground."
But on questions relating directly or indirectly to industrial growth
and operations, industrial interests (the Soviet equivalent of "economic
notables") come closer than do urban Party apparatchiki to constituting
a "ruling elite."

WHAT KIND OF PLURALISM?

How shall we characterize the political pluralism of Soviet
cities? Is it really the case, as H. Gordon Skilling puts it, that such
pluralism cannot be classified as "genuine"?[7] Is Andrew McFarland
correct to call it "spurious" because "one could say that the
administrators make unimportant routine decisions whereas the Party
makes the important critical decisions"? To readers of this book,
such judgments may appear strange. If, as McFarland defines them,
"important critical decisions are those made in constructing the
[Soviet] national economic plan, the comprehensive national budget
and in allocating crucial resources such as production equipment,"
then does not the urban evidence disprove his contention that "the
functionaries of the spuriously decentralized bureaucracy make only
unimportant, routine decisions"?[8]

Such questions drive us back to a basic problem: what are the
standards for identifying genuine, non-spurious pluralism? One
approach, developed by Dahl and Polsby, is to ask and answer the
following question: is there in the city any one small group, well-
defined and united in its policy aims, which consistently wins its way
on all or nearly all issues where other political actors prefer other
outcomes?[9] The answer in New Haven, according to Dahl and Polsby,
was no. Does the same answer not hold for Soviet cities? Neither
Party officials nor industrial managers—the two most likely

----

*It is worth recalling in this context the conclusions of B. Michael
Frolic cited in Chapter One: (1) "the basic fact of Party dominance
over urban decision making"; (2) the fact that "higher level authorities
decisively and consistently interfere in the municipal decision making
process" to the extent that "one wonders whether it is even appropriate
to speak of a Soviet municipal decision making process. . . ." See
Frolic, "Decision Making in Soviet Cities," p. 50.

candidates—pass this test. Instead these two powerful forces tend
to restrain each other. Ironically, centralization and Party power,
two elements that are usually seen as ensuring the elitist nature of
the Soviet system, contribute to making local pluralism possible.
Backing from superiors gives municipal officials at least some chance
to influence powerful industrial interests. Without the Party secretaries to rein them in, factory managers would indeed be able to accumulate sufficient power to qualify as a "ruling elite."

Should we not conclude then that Soviet pluralism is genuine?
Or is there something wrong with the Dahl-Polsby standard? Even
in the "posttotalitarian" era, many hesitate to recognize Soviet
pluralism as the genuine article. They would contend, with McFarland,
that such competition is spurious in comparison with American
politics, where "there is more bargaining by more people over more
important, more critical policy decisions."[10] What McFarland's line
of argument implies is another test—gauging not so much who in-
fluences whom but rather the importance of the issues. The contention is that, while relatively minor questions may be debated within
the limited bureaucratic framework of Soviet politics, truly important
issues are not permitted to arise. Which is, however, precisely the
charge made against American pluralism by writers who, in contrast
to Dahl and Polsby, view it as spurious.

The critique of American pluralism that I have in mind
encompasses a large and growing literature of which the neo-elitist
view of community power is a part. As summarized by William
Connolly, this school of thought makes a number of points: (1) that
"the prevailing system inhibits some segments of [American] society
from efficacious involvement while bestowing cumulative advantages
on others"; (2) that the "process of interest aggregation ignores some
concerns explicitly shared by many citizens because presistent, active
and legitimate 'groups' fail to define these concerns as high priority
interests"; and (3) that many latent concerns—those that may well
interest wide segments of society if they were publicly articulated
as issues—are not identified or sharply defined by the prevailing
system of issue formation."[11]

This is, of course, a controversial critique. How, for example,
to reconcile it with the argument, mentioned in our first chapter, that
far from exhibiting limited pluralism, American cities suffer from an
excess of same. One way to reconcile these two assessments
("limited" pluralism on the one hand, a surfeit on the other) is also
an avenue leading back to our Soviet subject. It is to say that both
evaluations apply in different issue areas, to say (taking a worst-of-
both-worlds approach) that there may exist both a tendency toward
stalemate on issues that are the subject of open competition, and a
"mobilization of bias" against major challenges to the status quo.

One who has explored this route is Theodore J. Lowi. His formulation
is that "when [American] public policy is facing the redistribution
of resources, the system is elitist in very much the theoretical and
empirical terms laid down by Mills and others." But when public
policy deals with "regulation" or with "distribution" of resources, then
one encounters varieties of "genuine" pluralist competition.[12]

It is not the business of this book to evaluate Lowi's formulation.
But Lowi does suggest, I believe, a potentially fruitful approach to
Soviet pluralism. McFarland is right when he contends that "there is
more bargaining by more people over more important, more critical
policy decisions" in the United States than in the USSR. All but the
most radical critics of American pluralism would agree with Connolly
that "the [American] mass media, although definitely biased, present
a significantly wider range of information and opinion"; that "freedoms
of association, assembly and speech are comparatively well protected
here . . . even after one has corrected for the gap between official
rhetoric and established practice."[13] Furthermore, whereas only
a few critics would accept the simplistic notion that an identifiable
power elite conspires to produce the bias of American pluralism, the
limits on Soviet dissent are established by the Party's all-too-visible
hand. But consider also Soviet issues on which debate is permitted.
Consider the fact that in recent years "on all but the most central
questions, Party policy is less and less incorporated into clear-cut
undebatable ideology," with the result, Jerry Hough continues, that
"there has, in fact, been virtually no conceivable proposal for incremental change in Party policy in the last five years which has not
been aired in the Soviet press."[14]

The fundamental Leninist principle of one-party rule, the Party
leadership's legitimacy, the innate and inevitable superiority of
Communism over capitalism—on such basic issues the Party brooks
no meaningful challenges. But on other issues—urban, environmental,
economic reforms—the picture is doubly different. Such issues are
the subject of a pluralist political struggle, which is inadequately
described by the term "spurious." And yet at the same time there is
an observable "mobilization of bias," which, far from deriving from
the Party's "monopoly of power," reflects the ability of vested
bureaucratic interests—in the urban case, entrenched industrial
interests—to resist the Party's efforts to encourage change.[15] What
such cases suggest is that Soviet pluralism is neither genuine nor
spurious, but rather, different and yet not so different; which in turn
suggests a reevaluation of the prospects for Soviet-American
convergence.

WHAT KIND OF CONVERGENCE?

The most familiar theory of convergence is optimistic.[16] It includes a hope—that the Soviet Union will open itself to a democratic political process while the United States musters the will and skill to plan and to allocate its resources in service of human needs. But the hope is based on an argument—that industrialization makes for an increasingly complex society, that a social pluralism provides the basis for political pluralism (genuine, of course), and that affluence weakens the fiber of authoritarian rule while education prepares its subject for democratic participation.

That theory—Isaac Deutscher was its founder—has often been debunked as naive.[17] Brzezinski and Huntington have called it "anti-Soviet Marxism: the forces of production will shape the social context of production, which in turn will determine the political superstructure."[18] Yet in recent years post-totalitarian analysts, including Brzezinski, have in effect resurrected the theory in the process of predicting the Soviet future in the "post-modern" era. Social differentiation, increasing economic and technological complexity—if such developments do not "require" democratic pluralist evolution, they at least ensure that the system that does not so evolve will pay a heavy price in loss of "effectiveness."[19]

There are, however, more pessimistic theories of convergence. One is James Burnham's vision of a "Managerial Revolution" triumphant in both East and West.[20] Another is Galbraith's view that in the Soviet Union as well as in the United States an "industrial system" is in the saddle and a technostructure rides mankind.[21] Similar too is Robert Heilbroner's warning that a new elitism may be "inherent in a society dominated by technology," and that the "the problem of maintaining the ecological balance, the very viability of the earth itself," poses to socialism the enormous challenge of imposing "stringent limitations not only on the productive apparatus of society" (which in the Soviet Union has for so long been favored) but "very possibly on its consumptive patterns," which are beginning to burst forth after being so long repressed.[22]

Different perspectives produce different views of the Soviet system. Most practicing Sovietologists would probably charge Galbraith with putting the managerial cart before the Party horse; they would counterpose Jeremy Azreal's conclusion that while

both American and Soviet societies have industrial
executives and in both societies economic leadership
entails political influence, . . . for the purposes of
political analysis, this similarity may be less significant

than the fact that group activities of the Soviet managerial
elite have never been accorded political legitimacy; that
members of the group have occupied bureaucratic positions within a centralized state system; that recruitment
into the managerial elite has been governed by political
criteria; . . . [emphasis added].[23]

In part such a difference concerning the power of industrialists
may reflect a terminological confusion as to who is included in the
category of managers. But the more important question is what is to
be considered more or less significant. True enough that on important
issues Soviet industrial managers have not won their way, and that
under Stalin a great many lost their lives in the process. It is also
true, however, that the system has given first priority to industrial
growth at the expense of other important goals—to the point that one
could argue that "surely the dominant forces of recent decades" have
been those, including managers and Party apparatchiki, which "empha-
size priority for industrial growth over other interests," including
balanced urban development.[24]

To those who are less fearful of managerial-technical elitism
or take a less apocalyptic view of environmental decay, Heilbroner's
warnings may ring hollow. And yet his and Galbraith's approach point
the way to important truths. Again one should be clear about
important distinctions. "In America," Daniel Bell has written, "no
one 'voted' for a new industrial society 200 years ago. . . . Yet a
whole new way of life, based on the utilitarian calculus or the
economizing mode gradually began to transform the whole of society."[25]
In the Soviet Union of the 1920s and 1930s the Party leadership could
and did make such a decision. Yet in the 1970s it is by no means
clear that the Party will be able to change direction to contain the
ill effects of industrial-technical progress, even assuming it desires
to do so.

For many the dream is still convergence. But those who are
not certain whether America will survive its racial conflict, its
generation gap, its environmental deterioration and urban decay, have
counterparts, such as Andrei Amalrik, who expects the USSR to
disintegrate as a multinational society in a war with China.[26] It
would be comforting to end on a hopeful note. But may not the two
societies (to judge by their cities, among other things) be moving
toward a different and more depressing commonality—the inability
to carry out the precedent-shattering changes that each so badly needs?
Despite everything, both will probably muddle through. Will that
constitute a triumph, or a disaster, or a little bit of each?

Between 1926 and 1959 the annual rate of growth of population in cities with more than 20,000 inhabitants was 0.71 percent, the fifth highest of 50 countries for which similar statistics are available. For these and other comparative statistics, see Cyril E. Black, "Soviet Society: A Comparative View," in Allen Kassoff, ed., Prospects for Soviet Society (New York: Frederick A. Praeger, 1968), p. 32.

POPULATION OF CITIES AND URBAN SETTLEMENTS IN 1926, 1959 AND 1970

City size by population	Over 500,000	100,000- 500,000	50,000- 100,000	20,000- 50,000	Under 20,000	Total
Number of cities of each size						
1926	3	28	60	135	1,699	1,925
1959	25	123	156	474	3,841	4,619
1970	33	188	188	599	4,496	5,504
Population of cities of each size (millions)						
1926	4.1	5.4	4.1	4.0	8.7	26.3
1959	24.2	24.4	11.0	14.8	25.6	100.0
1970	37.3	38.3	13.0	18.5	28.9	136.0
Number of cities of each size as a percent of total number						
1926	0.16	1.45	3.12	7.01	88.26	
1959	0.54	2.66	3.38	10.26	83.16	
1970	0.60	3.42	3.42	10.88	81.69	
Population of cities of each size as percent of total urban population						
1926	15.56	20.49	15.56	15.18	33.02	
1959	24.19	24.39	10.99	14.79	25.59	
1970	27.42	28.15	9.56	13.60	21.24	
Population of cities of each size as percent of total population						
1926	2.79	3.67	2.79	2.72	5.92	
1959	11.59	11.69	5.27	7.09	12.26	
1970	15.43	15.85	5.38	7.65	11.96	
Total population (millions)						
1926						147.0
1959						208.8
1970						241.7

Sources: Narodnoe khoziaistvo v SSSR V 1968 g.—statisticheskii ezhegodnik (The USSR national economy in 1968—statistical yearbook); "On the Preliminary Results of the All-Union Population Census," Pravda, April 19, 1970, pp. 1-2.

THE BUDGET-PLAN DRAFTING PROCESS[1]

To begin with there are the general directives for the national economic plan, established by the CPSU Central Committee and the USSR Council of Ministers. From these directives the USSR Ministry of Finance compiles guidelines on income and expenses for all-union agencies and republic ministries of finance. All-union ministries and state committees divide their allotted resources among their trusts and enterprises, and forward estimates on income and expenses to them. Republic finance ministries adapt guidelines to their areas and forward instructions to other republic ministries, to regional economic councils (in the years between 1957 and 1965), to departments of finance of province soviets and soviets of cities of republic subordination. These departments divide their estimated allotments among their own subordinates and send on further guidelines: ministries to their enterprises, economic councils to theirs, and soviet finance departments both to other departments of their own soviet and to finance departments of soviets below them. Each soviet department sends instructions to its enterprises.

When each enterprise, whatever its superior, has seen its instructions and drafted a budget, the "down process" is over and the "up process" begins. Enterprises send drafts to their superiors. The latter unite all budgets to make one draft budget for the entire ministry or soviet—but not for a city or province as such since no state organ at that level has authority over soviet and non-soviet enterprises. The next step, in theory, is for republic finance ministries to begin to compile the republic version based on planned economic indicators and previous performance. They do not even wait to receive local drafts before beginning, in that to wait would "drastically delay the drafting of republic and union budgets," and anyway, "a more detailed elaboration of local budgets is possible only after republic drafts are coordinated with those of all-union organizations."[2]

Eventually all drafts reach the USSR Ministry of Finance, which combines them into one USSR budget for presentation to the Council of Ministers, which presents the budget to the USSR Supreme Soviet, which, after making minor changes suggested by its standing committee, adopts it.

Finally the approved budget travels downward again. This time each agency that took part in the drafting process incorporates changes made higher up and sends final figures to its trusts and enterprises. Each soviet session now examines "its" budget for the first time and, employing the power reserved to it by law, ratifies the measure.

PREFACE

   1. L. Khripko, "The Trust and the City," Sovety deputatov trudiashchikhia (hereafter SDT) No. 3 (March 1966), p. 34.

   2. For an account of my year as an exchange student, see William Taubman, The View From Lenin Hills: Soviet Youth in Ferment (New York: Coward-McCann, 1967).

   3. The names of soviet executive committee chairmen and Party first secretaries of most important Soviet cities are listed in the Directory of Soviet Officials—Vol. I: USSR and RSFSR, U.S. Department of State, (Washington, D.C., 1966).

   4. As translated in Charlotte Saikowski and Leo Gruliow, eds., Current Soviet Policies IV: The Documentary Record of the 22nd Congress of the Communist Party of the Soviet Union (New York: Columbia University Press, 1962), p. 37.

CHAPTER 1

   1. Edward C. Banfield and James Q. Wilson, City Politics (New York: Random House, 1966), p. 1.

   2. For a survey of norms, see Iu. M. Kozlov, ed., Sovetskoe administrativnoe pravo (Soviet administrative law) (Moscow: Iuridicheskaia Literatura, 1964). More specific are articles in Mestnye sovety na sovremennom etape (Local soviets at present stage) (Moscow: Nauka, 1965); and a Moscow University text, G. V. Barabashev and K. F. Sheremet, Sovetskoe stroitel'stvo (Soviet affairs,) (Moscow: Iuridicheskaia Literatura, 1965). Unusually frank and revealing are V. A. Pertsik, Problemy mestnogo samoupravleniia v SSSR (Problems of local self-government in the USSR), Vol. XXXII, No. 6, Juridical Series entitled Trudy Irkutskogo gosudarstvennogo universiteta (Works of Irkutsk State University) (Irkutsk, 1963); and L. Karapetian and V. Razin, Sovety obshchena-rodnogo gosudarstva (Soviets of the all-peoples' state) (Moscow: Izdatel'svo Politicheskoi Literatury, 1964). The first book devoted solely to city government is B. N. Gabrichidze, Gorodskie sovety deputatov trudiashchikhsia (City soviets) (Moscow: Iuridicheskaia Literatura, 1968).

   Scholarly writing is particularly disappointing in view of the rich lode of material on political conflict that appears in the Soviet press; nor have experts in other disciplines filled the gap. Urban studies, as such, hardly existed until the late 1960s. Since then, though, interesting work has appeared in sociology, geography,

and urban planning. For a short survey, see B. Michael Frolic,
"The Soviet Study of Soviet Cities," Journal of Politics, 32, 3
(August 1970), 675-95.
    3. For an early exposition, see Carl J. Friedrich and Zbigniew
K. Brzezinski, Totalitarian Dictatorship and Autocracy (2nd ed.;
New York: Frederick A. Praeger, 1965). On "enlightened" or
"rationalized" post-Stalinist totalitarianism ("methods and policies"
changed but not "the substance of totalitarian power"), see Merle
Fainsod, How Russia Is Ruled (rev. ed.; Cambridge, Mass.: Harvard
University Press, 1963). The most complete study of local govern-
ment is Howard R. Swearer, "Local Government in the USSR: Public
Administration in a Totalitarian Society" (unpublished Ph.D. dissertation, Harvard University, 1960).
    4. Merle Fainsod, How Russia Is Ruled (Cambridge, Mass.:
Harvard University Press, 1953), p. 324.
    5. B. Michael Frolic, "Decision Making in Soviet Cities,"
American Political Science Review, LXVI, 1 (March 1972), 38-39,
50-51.
    6. In recent years, Western writers on Soviet cities have been
attempting new approaches, although not the one employed in this
book.
    Robert Osborn's 1962 Columbia University doctoral disser-
tation ("Public Participation in Soviet City Government: The Vision
of the Future in the Light of Current Problems of Urban Organization") studies relations between city and industrial agencies but
concentrated on voluntary citizens' groups. Robert Osborn, Soviet
Social Policies: Welfare Equality and Community (Homewood, Ill.:
Dorsey Press, 1970) includes perceptive chapters on urban development (pp. 187-265). David Cattell presents a straightforward
branch-by-branch survey of administration (but not, by and large,
politics) in Leningrad: A Case Study of Soviet Urban Government
(New York: Frederick A. Praeger, 1968). B. Michael Frolic
arrives ("The Soviet Study of Soviet Cities," p. 692) at a conclusion
that will strike readers of this book as strange: "Economic . . .
Notables hold some influence in North American cities, but none
in the USSR."
    7. See Chalmers Johnson, ed., Change in Communist Systems
(Stanford: Stanford University Press, 1970).
    8. Samuel P. Huntington, "Social and Institutional Dynamics of
One-Party Systems," in Samuel P. Huntington and Clement H. Moore,
Authoritarian Politics in Modern Society (New York: Basic Books,
1970), pp. 32-33.
    9. For two economists' evaluations, see Gregory Grossman,
"Economic Reforms: A Balance Sheet," Problems of Communism,
XV, 6 (November/December 1966), 43-61; and Gertrude E. Schroeder,

"Soviet Technology: System vs. Progress," Problems of Communism, XIX, 5 (September/October 1970), 19-29. Brzezinski develops his concept most fully in Between Two Ages: America's Role in the Technetronic Era (New York: Viking Press, 1970).

10. Zbigniew K. Brzezinski, "The Soviet Political System: Transformation or Degeneration," Problems of Communism, XV, 1 (January/February 1966), 15.

11. See, for example, Jerry F. Hough, The Soviet Prefects (Cambridge, Mass.: Harvard University Press, 1969), esp. chapters XIII-XV; and Frederic J. Fleron, Jr., "Toward a Reconceptualization of Political Change in the Soviet Union: The Political Leadership System," in Fleron, ed., Communist Studies and the Social Sciences: Essays on Methodology and Empirical Theory (Chicago: Rand McNally, 1969), pp. 222-43.

12. Huntington, "Social and Institutional Dynamics," p. 33.

13. For a study of the politics of pollution that reaches conclusions comparable to those of this book, see Marshall I. Goldman, The Spoils of Progress: Environmental Pollution in the Soviet Union (Cambridge, Mass.: M.I.T. Press, 1972).

14. J. K. Galbraith, The Affluent Society, (New York: Mentor Books, 1958), p. 103.

15. The concept of the industrial system is developed in Galbraith's The New Industrial State (New York: Signet Books, 1967). The quote is from p. 405.

16. Wallace S. Sayre and Herbert Kaufman, Governing New York City (New York: Russell Sage Foundation, 1960), pp. 710-12.

17. Theodore J. Lowi, The End of Liberalism: Ideology, Policy and the Crisis of Public Authority (New York: W. W. Norton, 1969), p. 193.

18. This is one conclusion of Francine Rabinovitz's City Planning and Politics (New York: Atherton Press, 1969). John W Dyckman describes "The Scientific World of the City Planners," The American Behavioral Scientist, VI, 6 (February 1963), pp. 46-50. For further discussion, see Alan Altshuler, The City Planning Process (Ithaca: Cornell University Press, 1965).

19. Sayre and Kaufman, Governing New York City, pp. 716-18.

20. For a conservative treatment, see Edward C. Banfield, The Unheavenly City (Boston: Little, Brown, 1970). For selected radical approaches, see William I. Connolly, ed., The Bias of Pluralism (New York: Atherton Press, 1969).

21. Logue spoke at a convocation, which took place at New York's Hilton Hotel on April 29, 1970. All quotations are from an unedited transcript kindly supplied by The Fund for Peace. Comparative cost figures, and the American official's comment, are cited in Ada Louise Huxtable's survey of Soviet architecture

in "Soviet Has Mastered the Industrialized Technology of Low Cost
Mass Building" The New York Times, October 20, 1967, p. 26.
22. "Soviet Architecture Assumes a New Look" The New York
Times, October 19, 1967, p. 26.
23. Huxtable, New York Times, October 20, 1967, p. 26.
24. For a short and cogent presentation of the Soviet governmental system and how it works, see John N. Hazard, The Soviet
System of Government (4th ed.; Chicago: University of Chicago
Press, 1968).
25. Ibid., p. 111.

CHAPTER 2
1. Allen Kassof, "The Administered Society: Totalitarianism
without Terror," World Politics, XVI, 4 (July 1964), 573.
2. In 1968 the American Council of Learned Societies convened
a Planning Group on the Comparative Study of Communism. Participants agreed, reported R. V. Burks, that "the totalitarian model
so much concentrates on the mechanism of control that no internal
change within the system seems possible, only its destruction from
the outside by superior forces." "Within the confines of the so-
called 'totalitarian model'," added Chalmers Johnson, "it is hard
enough to conceptualize 'development' and its consequences—that
is, to say at what rate a Communist regime is moving toward
achieving some or all of its self-proclaimed . . . goals. It is even
harder to conceptualize the resulting unintended changes in the
social structure and the consequences of those changes." Burks'
summary appears in "The ACLS Summer 1968 Workshop on the
Comparative Study of Communism: A Report," Newsletter on
Comparative Studies of Communism, II, 2 (June 1969), 2. Johnson's
judgment is in Johnson, "Comparing Communist Systems," in
Johnson, ed., Change in Communist Systems (Stanford: Stanford
University Press, 1970), p. 2.
3. Roger E. Kanet, ed., The Behavioral Revolution and Communist Studies (New York: The Free Press, 1971).
4. Truman's The Governmental Process: Public Interests
and Public Opinion was published in 1951; Bentley's pioneering
work, The Process of Government, was published in 1908. The
distinction between the two is drawn and discussed in Harry
Eckstein, "Group Theory and the Comparative Study of Pressure
Groups," in Harry Eckstein and David E. Apter, eds., Comparative
Politics: A Reader (New York: Free Press, 1963), pp. 389-96.
5. Harry Eckstein, "Group Theory," pp. 391-92. For a
summary of three lines of criticism, by a writer who proceeds
nonetheless to apply a group approach to the Soviet Union, see
Franklyn Griffiths, "A Tendency Analysis of Soviet Policy-Making,"

in H. Gordon Skilling and Franklyn Griffiths, eds., Interest Groups in Soviet Politics (Princeton: Princeton University Press, 1970), pp. 349-51.

6. Zbigniew Brzezinski and Samuel P. Huntington, Political Power: USA/USSR (New York: Viking Press, 1964), p. 196.

7. H. Gordon Skilling, "Groups in Soviet Politics: Some Hypotheses," in Skilling and Griffiths, eds., Interest Groups in Soviet Politics, pp. 24-25.

8. Earl Latham, "The Group Basis of Politics: Notes for a Theory," American Political Science Review, XLVI, 2 (June 1952), 384, n. 17.

9. Skilling, "Groups in Soviet Politics," p. 44.

10. Philip D. Stewart, "Soviet Interest Groups and the Policy Process: The Repeal of Production Education," World Politics, XXII, 1 (October 1969), 44.

11. Franklyn Griffiths, "A Tendency Analysis of Soviet Policy-Making," p. 336.

12. Andrew C. Janos, "Group Politics in Communist Society: A Second Look at the Pluralist Model," in Samuel P. Huntington and Clement H. Moore, Authoritarian Politics in Modern Society (New York: Basic Books, 1970), p. 446.

13. For Trotsky's views, see Leon Trotsky, The Revolution Betrayed (New York: Pioneer Publishers, 1945). A revisionist classic is Milovan Djilas, The New Class (New York: Frederick A. Praeger, 1957). General surveys are Fainsod, How Russia Is Ruled; John N. Hazard, The Soviet System of Government (4th ed.; Chicago: Chicago University Press, 1968); and Frederick C. Barghoorn, Politics in the USSR (Boston: Little, Brown, 1966). See also John Armstrong, The Soviet Bureaucratic Elite (New York: Frederick A. Praeger, 1959). Among the best accounts of bureaucracies in action (or inaction) are Joseph Berliner, Factory and Manager in the USSR (Cambridge, Mass.: Harvard University Press, 1957); Jeremy Azreal, Managerial Power and Soviet Politics (Cambridge, Mass.: Harvard University Press, 1966); and Jerry Hough, The Soviet Prefects (Cambridge, Mass.: Harvard University Press, 1969). Alfred G. Meyer proposes but does not himself fully flesh out a view of the Soviet political system as "one vast organization" in The Soviet Political System: An Interpretation (New York: Random House, 1965). Graham T. Allison offers guidelines for such an approach when he distinguishes, in a work on a very different subject, among (1) policy as "the realization of some purpose or intention," (2) policy that is the "output of organizational processes," and (3) policy that reflects intragovernmental bargaining; see Allison, Essence of Decision Explaining the Cuban Missile Crisis (Boston: Little, Brown, 1971).

14. "Observations on Bureaucracy, Totalitarianism, and the Comparative Study of Communism," in Fleron, ed., Communist Studies and the Social Sciences, p. 218.

15. Laws of bureaucratic behavior are drawn from the following: Graham T. Allison, Essence of Decision; Charles E. Lindblom, The Intelligence of Democracy (New York: The Free Press, 1965); David Braybrooke and Charles E. Lindblom, A Strategy of Decision (New York: The Free Press, 1963); Richard M. Cyert and James G. March, A Behavioral Theory of the Firm (Englewood Cliffs, N.J.: Prentice-Hall, 1963); Anthony Downs, Inside Bureaucracy (Boston: Little, Brown, 1967); James G. March and Herbert A. Simon, Organizations (New York: John Wiley, 1958); Herbert A. Simon, Donald W. Smithburg, and Victor A. Thompson, Public Administration (New York: Alfred A. Knopf, 1950); Gordon Tullock; The Politics of Bureaucracy (Washington, D.C.: Public Affairs Press, 1965); and Aaron Wildavsky, The Politics of the Budgetary Process (Boston: Little, Brown, 1964).

16. Tullock, The Politics of Bureaucracy, pp. 167-68.

17. Downs, Inside Bureaucracy, p. 159.

18. Ibid., pp. 165-66.

19. Study of the press and of Supreme Soviet sessions indicates that even leaders of Moscow and Leningrad did not press for changes—at least not in public—until 1957. See, for example, the speech of Moscow first secretary Ye. Furtseva, in Zasedaniia Verkhovnogo Soveta SSSR: stenograficheskii otchet (Meetings of the USSR Supreme Soviet: stenographic report) (hereafter abbreviated as USSR Zasedaniia), (4th call; 1st session; April 20-27, 1954), pp. 147-49; and the speech of N. I. Smirnov, Leningrad ispolkom chairman, in USSR Zasedaniia (4th call; 4th session; December 26-29, 1955), pp. 95-101.

CHAPTER 3

1. Conference proceedings were published as Vsesoiuznoe soveshchanie po gradostroitel'stvu 7-10 iunia, 1960: sokrashchenyi stenograficheskii otchet (All-union conference on urban development, June 7-10, 1960: condensed record) (Moscow: Gostroizdat, 1960).

2. Ibid., pp. 10-14.

3. Quoted in Jerry F. Hough, The Soviet Prefects (Cambridge, Mass.: Harvard University Press, 1969), p. 269.

4. B. Svetlichnyi (deputy director, Department of Housing, Municipal Services and Urban Development, USSR Gosplan), "Urban Development and City Planning," Arkhitektura SSSR, No. 3 (March 1966), p. 29. Hough reports (The Soviet Prefects, p. 269) that in 1967 only 2 percent of State Planning Commission personnel were engaged in territorial planning.

5. This catalogue of shortcomings is compiled from the following: V. Kucherenko, "Several Questions of Soviet Urban Development," Pravda, June 1, 1960, pp. 2-3; B. Svetlichnyi, "Soviet City Planning at the Present Stage," Voprosy ekonomiki, No. 7 (July 1960), pp. 52-59; and Robert J. Osborn and Thomas A. Reiner, "Soviet City Planning," Journal of the American Institute of Planners, XXVII, 4 (November 1962), 239-50.

6. For an orthodox view, see B. Svetlichnyi, "The City Awaits a Reply," Oktiabr', No. 10 (October 1966), pp. 157-69. On doubts about that view that appeared in the 1960s, see Robert J. Osborn, Soviet Social Policies (Homewood, Ill.: Dorsey Press, 1970) pp. 199-209. For further discussion, see Chapter 8 of this book.

7. D. Valentei (director of the Moscow University of Population Problems) and B. Khorev (laboratory sector head), "The Problems of Cities," Ekonomicheskaia gazeta, No. 29 (July 1967), p. 18.

8. See Moscow: General Plan of Reconstruction of the City (Moscow: Union of Soviet Architects, 1935), p. 38. The passport system is described in E. D. Simon and others, Moscow in the Making (London: Longmans, Green, 1937), p. 199.

9. Narodnoe khoziaistvo SSSR v 1964: staticheskii ezhegodnik (The USSR national economy in 1964: statistical yearbook) (Moscow, 1965), p. 32. For a more complete picture of urban population growth patterns, see Appendix A.

10. Documentation for these statements is in Chapters 7 through 10. For additional statistics, see Timothy Sosnovy, "The Soviet City," in Dimensions of Soviet Economic Power, Joint Economic Committee, United States Congress, 87th Congress, 2nd Session, (Washington, D.C., 1963), pp. 325-45; and Sosnovy, "Housing Conditions and Urban Development," pp. 535-53.

11. For a more complete treatment of the Bolsheviks' urban inheritance and their early city planning experience, see the book on which this section is largely based—M. F. Parkins, City Planning in Soviet Russia (Chicago: University of Chicago Press, 1953).

12. Ibid., p. 5.

13. Robert Osborn examines the Bolshevik approach, its roots in Marxism, and its place in the context of Western approaches to city planning, in Osborn, Soviet Social Policies, pp. 187-96.

14. Parkins, City Planning, p. 15.

15. Svetlichnyi, "Urban Development and City Planning," p. 31.

16. I am indebted to Professor Alexander Erlich for this observation.

17. Svetlichnyi, "The City Awaits a Reply," as translated in Current Digest of the Soviet Press (hereafter CDSP), XVIII, 48 (1966), 11.

18. Vsesoiuznoe soveshchanie, p. 11.

19. Osborn, Soviet Social Policies, p. 200.

20. Ibid. pp. 224-225. Describing the Industrial Revolution in England, David Landes notes a roughly similar phenomenon. Because housing investment's capital-output ratio is so high (Landes incorrectly calls it "infinite"), housing "represents a heavy burden for an industrializing capital-poor society." See Landes, "The Industrial Revolution: 1750-1850," in Chapters in Western Civilization, Vol. II (New York: Columbia University Press, 1962), p. 187.

21. Albert O. Hirschman, The Strategy of Economic Development (New Haven: Yale University Press), p. 93.

22. Ibid., p. 95.

23. "On the Development of Housing Construction in the USSR," July 31, 1957. Excerpts are in Zhilishchnobytovye voprosy: sbornik rukovodiashchikh materialov (Problems of housing and everyday services: collected rulings) (Moscow: Profizdat, 1964), p. 9. The rights of zakazchik and other parties to a construction contract are outlined in Iuridicheskii spravochnik khoziaistvennika (Legal handbook for the manager) (Moscow: Izdatel'stvo Moskovskogo Universiteta, 1963), pp. 219-38.

24. The decree's provisions are noted in M. Vershinin, "Protect Housing-The National Property," SDT, No. 7 (July 1961), p. 17.

25. The change took place as part of the major 1957 reform, which abolished most ministries and turned industrial administration over to regional economic councils. The description is in V. Chkhikvadze, I. Pavlov, and I. Azovkin, "Increasing the Role of Soviets is an Immediate Task," SDT, No. 8 (August 1965), p. 15. Local industries produced, among other things, construction materials, bread, beer, soft drinks, and milk and butter products. In the RSFSR, local soviets (province and district as well as city) received more than 3,400 enterprises; in the Ukraine, the corresponding figure was 767. For these and other statistics, see I. Azovkin, "The Development of the Material-Financial Base and of the Competence of Local Soviets," in Mestnye Sovety na sovremennom etape (Moscow: Nauka, 1965), p. 62.

26. Pravda March 15, 1958, p. 2.

27. Cited in Osborn, Soviet Social Policies, p. 203.

28. For a standard discussion of the Soviet policy-making process, see Zbigniew Brzezinski and Samuel P. Huntington, Political Power: USA/USSR (New York: Viking Press, 1964), pp. 202-23.

29. The resolution, dated January 22, 1957, and entitled "On Improving the Work of Soviets and Strengthening Their Links with the Masses," is in Bor'ba KPSS za zavershenie stroitel'stva sotsializma (The struggle of the CPSU for the completion of the building of socialism) (Moscow: Gospolitizdat, 1961), pp. 487-89.

30. Noted by V. F. Promyslov, deputy chairman of the Moscow City Soviet, in a speech to the CPSU Central Committee Plenum of June 24-29, 1959. See Plenum Tsentral'nogo Komiteta Kommunisticheskoi Partii Sovetskogo Soiuza: stenograficheskii otchet (Plenum of the Central Committee of the Communist Party of the Soviet Union: stenographic report) (hereafter abbreviated as Plenum CC), June 24-29, p. 617.

31. For discussion of incentive funds, see Z. A. Tkach, "Applying the Statute on the Socialist State Production Enterprise," Sovetskoe gosudarstvo i pravo (hereafter SGP), No. 1 (January 1967), p. 90; and K. Martynov, "Experience With the New System of Planning and Economic Incentives," SGP, No. 5 (May 1967), pp. 98-103.

32. Chkhikvadze, Pavlov, and Azovkin, "Increasing the Role of the Soviets," p. 15. The cities of Sverdlovsk and Ufa are added to the formula by G. Barabashev, K. Sheremet, and P. Titov, "The Role of the Soviets in the Development of the Socialist Economy," SDT, No. 12 (December 1965), p. 19.

33. See Iu. A. Tikhomirov, "The Development of the Democratic Bases of the Organization and Activities of Local Soviet Organs," Mestnye sovety, p. 34.

34. For overall urbanization pattern, see Appendix A. For specific cities, see "On the Preliminary Results of the 1970 All-Union Population Census," Pravda, April 19, 1970, pp. 1-2.

35. The Central Committee resolution, in Pravda, March 14, 1971, pp. 1-2, was translated in CDSP, XXIII, 11 (1971), 1-5. The Supreme Soviet decree, in Izvestiia, March 20, 1971, p. 4, is also in CDSP, XXIII, 13 (1971), 27-30. The Council of Ministers resolution, in Pravda, March 20, 1971, p. 1, is also in CDSP, XXIII, 11, 5.

36. Supreme Soviet decree in CDSP, XXIII, 13, 27.

37. Central Committee resolution in CDSP, XXIII, 11, 4.

CHAPTER 4

1. For a general treatment of the role of executive committees, see G. V. Barabashev and K. F. Sheremet, Sovetskoe stroitel'stvo (Moscow: Iuridicheskaia Literatura, 1965) pp. 232-47. On the importance of chairmen, see David T. Cattell, Leningrad: A Case Study of Soviet Urban Government (New York: Frederick A. Praeger, 1968), p. 32.

2. Barabashev and Sheremet, Sovetskoe stroitel'stvo, p. 32.

3. The rights listed are those specified in the Ukraine statute on city soviets, which is included in A. G. Khazikov, Sbornik normativnykh aktov po sovetskomu administrativnomu pravu

(Collected administrative law statutes) (Moscow: Vyshaia Shkola, 1964), p. 79. For a discussion of other republic statutes and the variations among them, see Barabashev and Sheremet, Sovetskoe stroitel'stvo, p. 168.

4. Sorok let sovetskogo prava II (Forty years of soviet law) Leningrad, 1957, p. 20.

5. As described, for example, in V. I. Nizhechek, "Sochetanie gosudarstvennykh i obshchestvennykh nachal v organizatsii i deiatel'nosti mestnykh sovetov deputatov trudiashchikhsia," (The combination of state and non-state principles in the organization and activities of local soviets of workers' deputies) (unpublished Kandidat dissertation, Irkutsk State University, 1963), p. 102.

6. Evidence of deputies' powerlessness is cited by Iu. A. Tikhomirov and R. A. Safarov, in their contributions to Mestnye sovety na sovremmenom etape (Moscow: Nauka, 1965), pp. 150, 159, 163, 183. More details on Party control over the city soviet are given in in Chapter 6 of this book.

7. Barabashev and Sheremet, Sovetskoe stroitel'stvo, p. 200. For a statute regulating commissions in Irkutsk, see Uchastie obshchestvennosti v rabote mestnykh sovetov (Participation by the public in the work of local soviets) (Irkutsk, 1964), pp. 4-11.

8. G. Petrov, "On the Form and Content of New Laws," SDT, No. 6 (June 1967), p. 85.

9. L. Karapetian and V. Razin, Sovety obshchenarodnogo gosudarstva (Moscow: Izdatel'stvo Politicheskoi Literatury, 1964), p. 70.

10. A. Selivanov and D. Ustimenko, "Important Tasks of the Executive Committees of the District Soviets," Biulleten' Ispolnitel'-nogo Komiteta Moskovskogo Gorodskogo Soveta Deputatov Trudiash-chikhsia (hereafter abbreviated as Bulletin-Moscow, No. 4 (February 1966), p. 18.

11. B. M. Lazarev, cited in Gabrichidze, Gorodskie sovety deputatov trudiashchikhsia (Moscow: Iuridicheskaia Literatura, 1968), p. 193.

12. Arutunian, "Both All-Union and Republic. . . ," pp. 70-71.

13. "What Should the Statutes on Local Soviets Say?" SDT, No. 8 (August 1966), p. 48.

14. See, for example, "On Horizontal Subordination," SDT, No. 2 (February 1967), p. 76.

15. This particular list is based on Pertsik, Problemy mestnogo samoupravleniia v SSSR, Vol. XXXII, No. 6, Juridical Series entitled Trudy Irkutskogo Universiteta (Irkutsk, 1963), pp. 130-31. For a more complete treatment see Sovetskoe finansovoe pravo (Soviet Financial Law) (Moscow: Iuridichesaia Literatura, 1961).

16. Frolic, "The Soviet Study of Soviet Cities," p. 690.

17. Pertsik, Problemy, p. 132.

CHAPTER 5

1. The statutes, as well as scholars' different interpretations of them, are described in Ts. A. Iampol'skaia, A. V. Luzhin, and A. S. Pribluda, eds., Pravovye voprosy organizatsii i deiatel'nosti sovnarkhozov (Legal aspects of the organization and activities of economic councils) (Moscow: Izdatel'stvo Akademii Nauk SSSR, 1961), pp. 302-12. The Azerbaijan city soviet statute is translated in Harold J. Berman and John B. Quigley Jr., eds., Basic Laws on the Structure of the Soviet State (Cambridge, Mass.: Harvard University Press, 1969), pp. 142-63.

2. Azovkin, "Material-Financial Base," p. 119.

3. Arutunian, "Both All-Union and Republic. . . ," p. 69.

4. B. Gabrichidze and M. Shafir, "Soviet and Enterprise," Izvestiia, October 16, 1966, p. 3.

5. See B. Svetlichnyi, "Urban Development and City Planning," Arkhitektura SSSR, No. 3 (March 1966), pp. 28-32.

6. See the decree, "On Procedures for Ratifying Draft Plans for City Construction," August 24, 1955, as summarized in T. Alekseev, "Procedures for Construction and Acceptance of Apartment Houses and Other Buildings," SDT, No. 1 (January 1959), pp. 94-96.

7. Decree of the RSFSR Council of Peoples' Commissars, "On Measures for Fighting Arbitrary Construction in Cities and in Workers' Resort and Vacation Settlements," May 22, 1940; and Instruction of the RSFSR Peoples' Commissariat of Municipal Services, "On the Procedure for Granting Land Allotments for Construction in Cities and Workers' Settlements," April 16, 1941; both statutes in I. N. Andreevskii, ed., Spravochnik po zakonodatel'-stvy dlia rabotnikov zhilishchno kommunal'nogo khoziaitsva (Handbook on legislation for workers in housing-municipal services) (Moscow: Stroizdat, 1964), pp. 61-67.

8. Relevant laws are (1) Decree of the USSR Council of Ministers, "On Procedures for Accepting Completed Construction," September 15, 1962; and (2) Decree of RSFSR Council of Ministers, "On Procedures for Accepting Completed Construction of Housing and Other Buildings in Cities, and Workers' and Resort Settlements in the RSFSR," September 7, 1946; both statutes in Andreevskii, ed., Spravochnik, pp. 339-41. Quotation is on p. 341.

9. Decree of the Presidium of the USSR Supreme Soviet, "On Further Limitation of the Use of Fines Imposed in Administrative Procedure," June 21, 1961, in Administrativnye shtrafy: sbornik normativnykh aktov (Administrative fines: collected legislation)

(Moscow: Iuridicheskaia Literatura, 1965), pp. 3-12. Ordinances
enacted by city soviets cover all aspects of city life. Moscow
ordinances filled 466 pages of an official manual in 1941—Sbornik
obiazatel'nykh postanovlenii i reshenii ispolnitel'nogo komiteta
Moskovskogo gorodskogo soveta (Collected obligatory decrees and
decisions of the Moscow City Soviet) (Moscow: Moskovskii
Rabochii, 1941). Contemporary examples may be found in Bulletin-
Moscow. "On Maintenance of Cleanliness and Order in the City of
Moscow," which sets standards for non-city as well as city agencies
and ordinary citizens, is in Bulletin-Moscow, No. 14 (July 1964),
pp. 11-14. A ruling reprimanding non-city enterprises for not
repairing their housing, and warning them to remedy the situation
or face fines, is in Bulletin-Moscow, No. 3 (February 1966), pp.
6-8. The enterprise device of including fine money in the plan is
noted by V. Parfenov, "How Much Does a Liter of Water Cost?"
Pravda, May 21, 1966, p. 4.

10. Fundamental rules of housing distribution are established
in Article 56 of "Bases of Civil Legislation of the USSR and the
Union Republics," as approved by the USSR Supreme Soviet on
December 8, 1961 and amended by its Presidium on November 9,
1966 (see also RSFSR Civil Code Article 296). The pre-1965 rules
are interpreted, with citations of other relevant laws, in S. Rozantsev,
Sto otvetov na voprosy po zhilishchnomu zakonodatel'stvu (One
Hundred Answers to Questions on Housing Law) (Moscow: Profizdat,
1965); see especially pages 5-15. The key document spelling out
the 1965 reform was the Decree of the CPSU Central Committee
and the USSR Council of Ministers, "On the Improvement of Planning
and the Strengthening of Economic Incentives in Industrial Production," October 4, 1965. The post-1965 regulations were adapted to
Moscow conditions by a decision of the Moscow Executive Committee on December 24, 1966; cited in Bulletin-Moscow, No. 4
(February 1967), pp. 16-18.

11. Sovetskoe finansovoe pravo, p. 139.

12. As reported by B. Michael Frolic.

13. Supreme Soviet decree in Izvestiia, March 20, 1971, p. 4.

14. Pre-1965 central controls are described in the following:
Decree of the USSR Council of Ministers, "On Enterprise Funds
for the Improvement of Cultural and Everyday Services for Workers
and for Improvement of Production," February 4, 1961, cited in
Andreevskii, ed., Spravochnik, pp. 143-44; and Decree of the RSFSR
Council of Ministers, "On the Regulation of Above-plan Spending
on Capital Construction Financed by Non-centralized Resources,"
July 23, 1960, in Andreevski, ed., op. cit., p. 309.

15. The 1965 Statute on Socialist State Production Enterprises
is translated in CDSP, XVII, 42 (1965), 5. The reform divided

enterprise funds into three separate funds: (1) Fund for Social-
Cultural Measures and Housing Construction; (2) Fund for Material
Incentive; (3) Fund for Production.

16. See, for example, V. A. Acharkan (of the Scientific Research
Institute on Labor of the USSR State Committee on Labor and Pay),
"Legal Regulations on the Use of Funds for Social-Cultural Measures
and Housing Construction," SGP, No. 4 (April 1967), p. 46.

CHAPTER 6

1. G. V. Barabashev and K. F. Sheremet, Sovetskoe stroitel'-
stvo (Moscow: Iuridicheskaia Literatura, 1965), p. 72.

2. Internal Party politics is not open to outside observers,
but hints in the Soviet press plus recent American studies of Soviet
local government suggest a pattern probably applicable to most
cities. Such studies include, in addition to those already mentioned,
Philip D. Stewart, Political Power in the Soviet Union: A Study of
Decision-Making in Stalingrad (New York: Bobbs-Merrill, 1968).

3. Stewart, Political Power in the Soviet Union, p. 86.

4. The names of bureau members are in Directory of Soviet
Officials, U.S. Department of State, Revisions to February 1966
Edition, pp. II-C3 and II-C9. Biographical information on members
is in Who's Who in the USSR—1965/1966 (Montreal: Intercontinental
Book and Publishing Company, 1966), and in Prominent Personalities
in the USSR—1968 (Metuchen, N.J.; The Scarecrow Press, 1968).
There seems no reason to doubt that in smaller cities, Party
professionals, though fewer, form the majority in smaller bureaus.

5. "On Improving the Work of Soviets and Strengthening Their
Links with the Masses," January 22, 1957, in Bor'ba KPSS za
zavershenie stroitel'stva sotsializma (Moscow: Gospolitizdat,
1961), p. 493.

6. CPSU Central Committee, "On the Work of Local Soviets
in Poltava Province," Partiinaia zhizn', No. 23 (December 1965),
p. 19.

7. David T. Cattell, "Leningrad: A Case Study of Soviet Local
Government," Western Political Quarterly XVII, 2 (June 1964), 195.

8. See, for example, a report on Tashkent in SDT, No. 8
(August 1958), p. 85.

9. Cattell, "Leningrad: A Case Study of Soviet Local Government," p. 195.

10. Voprosy partiinogo stroitel'stva (Problems of Party work)
(3 vols.; Leningrad: Lenizdat, 1960-65), II, p. 664.

11. Ustav kommunisticheskoi partii Sovetskogo soiuza (Rules
of the Communist Party of the Soviet Union) (Moscow: Politizdat,
1965), Statute 59, p. 27.

12. Moscow Executive Committee members are listed in Bulletin-Moscow, No. 6 (March 1965), p. 18. On Leningrad, see Cattell, Leningrad: A Case Study of Soviet Urban Government, p. 40.

13. Cattell, "Leningrad," p. 196.

14. B. I. Bartyshev, "Kompetentsiia raionnogo soveta deputatov trudiashchikhsia na sovremennom etape" (The competence of district soviets at the present stage) (unpublished Kandidat dissertation, Moscow State University, 1965), p. 51.

15. Personal interview.

16. Voprosy partiinogo stroitel'stva, II, p. 665.

17. D. Polyansky, "Recruitment and Training of Cadres," SDT, No. 2 (August 1957), p. 19. It is interesting to note that in 1957 Polyansky cited the authority of Chairman Mao Tse-tung on how to inspire ineffective cadres.

18. Editorial in Pravda, February 23, 1953, as cited in Jerry F. Hough, "The Soviet Concept of the Relationship Between the Lower Party Organs and the State Administration," Slavic Review, XXIV, 2 (June 1965), 228.

19. See Jerry F. Hough, The Soviet Prefects (Cambridge, Mass.: Harvard University Press, 1969) on the evidence and conclusions on which this section is largely based. Hough concentrates on province Party committees and industrial decision making, but Party gorkoms can use similar weapons in disputes concerning urban developments.

20. Personal interview with a professor of state and law.

21. Voprosy partiinogo stroitel'stva, Vol. I. p. 344.

22. Ibid., Vol. II, p. 338.

23. Hough, "The Soviet Concept," p. 228.

24. Voprosy partiinogo stroitel'stva, Vol. III, p. 457.

25. Jerry F. Hough, "The Role of Local Party Organs in Soviet Industrial Decision Making," (unpublished Ph.D. dissertation, Harvard University, 1961), pp. 123,273.

CHAPTER 7

1. Quoted in M. F. Parkins, City Planning in Soviet Russia (Chicago: University of Chicago Press, 1953), p. 33.

2. Dates of founding and levels of subordination for all cities in this and subsequent sections are in SSSR: Administrativno-territorial'nye delenii soiuznykh respublik (USSR: Administrative-territorial divisions of union-Republics) (Moscow, 1965). The 1970 population figures were reported in Pravda, April 19, 1970, pp. 1-2.

3. Soviet Life (May 1968), p. 2.

4. Ernst May, "Cities of the Future," in Walter Laqueur and Leopold Labedz, eds., The Future of Soviet Society (New York: Frederick A. Praeger, 1962), p. 182. For a complete history of Magnitogorsk, see V. I. Kazarinova and V. I. Pavlichenkov, Magnitogorsk (Moscow: Izdatel'stvo Literatury po Stroitelstvu, Arkhitekture i Stroitel'nym Materialam, 1961).

5. The story of Magnitogorsk's troubles made the headlines in 1960. The first major expose was I. Drozdov, "A City without a Master," Izvestiia, October 20, 1960, p. 3. Further details followed in N. Shcherinov (deputy to the Magnitogorsk City Soviet), "Put the City Economy into One Pair of Hands," SDT, No. 6 (June 1961), pp. 69-71. These articles, which agree on all main points, are cited below only to identify direct quotations. Other sources are noted as cited.

6. See Drozdov, "A City without a Master."

7. Vladimir Chivilikhin, "How is Your Breathing City Dwellers?" Literaturnaia gazeta, August 9, 1967, p. 10, as translated in CDSP, XIX, No. 33 (1967), p. 10.

8. Shcherinov, "Put the City Economy into One Pair of Hands," p. 70.

9. See V. Parfenov, "How Much Does a Liter of Water Cost?" Pravda, May 21, 1966, p. 4.

10. Shcherinov, "Put the City Economy into One Pair of Hands," p. 70.

11. Ibid., p. 71.

12. See Drozdov, "A City without a Master."

13. Province authorities reported their agreement with Shcherinov in A. Kardanol'tsev (chairman of the Cheliabinsk Province Executive Committee) and A. Rozhdestvenski (secretary of the executive committee), "Here There Will Be a Master," Izvestiia, June 28, 1961, p. 3.

14. Reported in Drozdov, "A City without a Master."

15. Izvestiia expressed its views in two editorials: "Caring about the Plan, Caring about People," April 4, 1961, p. 1; and "The Soviet—Master of the City," September 15, 1961, p. 1. Shcherinov's article in Sovety deputatov also appeared at this time. The government's decision was reported in SDT, No. 11 (November 1961), p. 77.

16. I. Bosenko, (chairman, Magnitogorsk City Soviet), "In One Pair of Hands," Izvestiia, February 1, 1970, p. 3.

17. Quoted in A. Ozerskii, "In a Young City," SDT, No. 4 (October 1957), p. 82.

18. Quoted in A. Sryvtsev, "Problems of Construction in a Big City," SDT, No. 10 (October 1959), p. 62. Another source recalls that early houses were built in the lee of factory

smokestacks, which, nearly circling the city, formed an almost
complete ring of pollution. After the war, central ministries
constructed two plants that closed the ring entirely. See B.
Svetlichnyi, "The City Awaits a Reply," Oktiabr', No. 10 (October
1966) as translated in CDSP, XVIII, No. 48 (1966), p. 15.

19. Ozerskii, "In a Young City," p. 80.

20. Ibid., p. 81.

21. Ibid., p. 80.

22. V. Davydchenkov and Iu. Feofanov, "The City and Its Soviet,"
Izvestiia, January 26, 1961, p. 3.

23. SDT, No. 10 (October 1965), p. 46.

24. See A. Rozhkov, "On City Government," SDT, No. 7 (July
1968), pp. 74-77.

25. Statistics are cited in B. Svetlichnyi, "Long Life for Apartment Houses!" SDT, No. 12 (December 1967), pp. 26-27.. Another
source (Vershinin, "Protect Housing," p. 17) attributes the difference to industry's habit of "looking at housing as a profitless
business, treating it like some black sheep, stinting on funds for
capital repair."

26. See, for example, N. Komkov, "Some Problems in Municipal
Services," SDT, No. 6 (December 1957), p. 24. An Institute of State
and Law scholar once summed up local soviet shortcomings as:
"formalism, inertia, old-fashioned attitudes, a tendency to wait
for orders from above and to issue vague mandates instead of
specific instructions." See I. Azovkin, "The Development of the
Material-Financial Base and of the Competence of Local Soviets,"
Mestnye Sovety na sovre mennom etape (Moscow: Nauka, 1965),
p. 113.

27. P. Mostovoi, "City and Factory," Izvestiia, July 7, 1965,
p. 3. Except where noted otherwise, this account of Kramatorsk
is based on Mostovoi's article.

28. K. F. Sheremet made this point at an expanded session of
the Scientific Council of the Institute of State and Law in May 1967.
Present at the session were scholars, local soviet officials, and
representatives of the Presidia of the USSR and RSFSR supreme
soviets. Participants discussed the findings of institute researchers
in Kazakhstan and Estonia, recognized the need for an all-union statute on city government that would bolster soviets' rights, and called
for increases in soviet staffs and sources of independent income.
The session is described in SGP, No. 8 (August 1967), p. 139.

29. I. Polushin, "Your City is Not Municipal," Izvestiia,
February 12, 1960, p. 4.

30. Iu. Feofanov and S. Morozov, "Smiles and Grimaces,"
Izvestiia, July 19, 1961, p. 3.

31. See V. Antonov and E. Grishaev, "Who is the Master in
Krivoi Rog?" SDT No. 4 (April 1960), p. 75-80.
32. See V. Rumiantsev, "Why Must They Supplant?" SDT,
No. 11 (November 1965), p. 64. Rumiantsev, a borough Party
committee functionary, admits that, ideally, the Party committee
should limit itself to "encouraging city officials to be more ener-
getic, imaginative and demanding." But he claims that only one-
third of the issues involving intervention by the Party committee
could have been decided by the soviet alone. The rest, many
involving stubborn non-city agencies, did indeed require Party
action.
33. "The Soviet Is Master of the City." Izvestiia, September
15, 1961, p. 1.
34. K. Lagunov, "A Town Is Being Built in the Taiga," Pravda,
October 22, 1969, p. 3.
35. This account is based on N. Churakov, "The Assertion of
Power," SDT, No. 12 (December 1967), pp. 81-85.
36. Ibid., p. 82.
37. Ibid., p. 84.
38. Ibid.
39. A. Murzin, "Letters from Western Siberia," Pravda, March
8, 1970, p. 2.
40. See I. Serikov, "Attention: A City Is Being Born," SDT,
No. 9 (September 1965), pp. 38-42.
41. Ibid., pp. 39-40.
42. Ibid., p. 41.
43. Ibid., p. 42.
44. SDT, No. 2 (February 1966), p. 90.

CHAPTER 8
1. S. Isliukov (Chuvash Autonomous Province), "The Large
Problems of Small Cities," SDT, No. 6 (June 1966), p. 24.
2. The other 50 percent of output is produced in 892 cities
and 1,841 urban-type settlements. See M. Mkrtchian, "Methodological Questions of the Geographical Distribution of Productive Forces, "
Planovoe Khoziaistvo, No. 12 (December 1969), pp. 36-45, as
translated in CDSP, XXII, 6 (1970), 6.
3. S. Trubnikov, "Consumer Services and the Problem of
Personnel," Planovoe Khoziaistvo, No. 5 (May 1968), pp. 22-23,
as translated in Current Abstracts of the Soviet Press I, No. 4
(1968), p. 9.
4. Robert J. Osborn, Soviet Social Policies, p. 229.
5. This account is based on I. Serikov, "The Just Cause of
the Metallurgists," SDT, No. 10 (October 1965), pp. 38-42; and
V. Gin'ko, "The Concern of Small Cities," Izvestiia, March 15,
1966, p. 3.

6. Serikov, "The Just Cause of the Metallurgists," p. 39.

7. Gin'ko, "The Concern of Small Cities."

8. Quotation is from Izvestiia's introduction to A. Ivakin (chairman of the Piatigorsk City Soviet), "The City Soviet and the Agencies," Izvestiia, June 9, 1965, p. 3. Ivakin's letter describes the situation in Piatigorsk.

9. This account is based on A. Fesenko, "The Chief Architect," SDT, No. 8 (August 1965), pp. 75-79.

10. Ibid., p. 78.

11. Ibid., pp. 77-78.

12. Ibid., p. 79.

13. I. Levishchev (chairman, Aiaguz City Soviet), "The City of District Subordination," SDT, No. 3 (March 1958), pp. 74-77.

14. SDT, No. 8 (August 1958), p. 82.

15. For letter by the mayor of Karataly, see SDT, No. 8 (August 1958), p. 82.

16. On Stepniak (in Kazakhstan), see the mayor's letter in SDT, No. 9 (September 1960), pp. 77-80. The letter from the chairman of Novoukrainsk appears in SDT, No. 1 (January 1964), pp. 100-102.

17. T. Bechavia, "Who is the Master of Gagra?" SDT, No. 3 (March 1967), pp. 33-36.

18. Ibid., p. 36.

19. 1940; @15,000, Leningrad province. V. Negri, "If You Cannot Do It, Do Not Promise To; If You Promised, Do It." Izvestiia, May 30, 1968, p. 3.

20. Svetlichnyi, "City Awaits a Reply," Oktiabr', No. 10 (October 1966), as translated in CDSP, VIII, No. 48 (1966), p. 12.

21. V. Seliunin, "Our Daily Work," Moskva, No. 7 (July 1967), pp. 173-86, as translated in CDSP, XIX, No. 38 (1967), p. 10.

22. See Valentei and Khorev, "The Problem of the Cities," p. 18.

23. V. Perevedentsev, "What Kind of City is Advantageous," Literaturnaia gazeta, September 20, 1967, p. 11, as translated in CDSP, XIX, No. 38 (1967), p. 6.

24. V. Perevedentsev, "The Future of the Small City," Literaturnaia gazeta, January 17, 1968, p. 11, as translated in CDSP, XX, No. 3 (1968), p. 10.

25. For a brief summary of the debate, including one planner's comment that Perevedentsev is fascinated with "Western bourgeois ideas" and is "a sloppy scholar," see Frolic, "The Soviet Study of Soviet Cities," pp. 684-86. Also see Osborn, Soviet Social Policies, pp. 207-209. The calculation concerning cost of municipal services comes from Moscow University's Laboratory of Population Problems and is reported by Valentei and Khorev in "The Problem of Cities."

26. Inessa Burkova, "Kuzma," Literaturnaia Rossiia, May 6, 1966, pp. 16-17, as translated in CDSP, XVII, No. 19 (1966), pp. 16-19.

CHAPTER 9

1. M. Mkrtchian, "Methodological Questions of the Geographic Distribution of Productive Forces," Planovoe khoziastvo, No. 12 (December 1969) as translated in CDSP XXII, No. 6 (1970), p. 31.

2. Ibid., p. 7.

3. B. Tutkarin, (chairman, East Kazakhstan Province Soviet Executive Committee) "Local Interest," Pravda, May 8, 1969, p. 3. Tutkarin continues as follows: "During the early five-year-plans era, the conviction was formed that everything could be sacrificed for the sake of production. While people were sinking mine-shafts and building plants they were living in mud-huts and barracks. At that time there was no need to explain why sacrifices had to be made. The undeniable rule 'everything for production' has caused great imbalances in urban development. But today the times are quite different."

4. Mkrtchian, "Methodological Questions . . .," p. 31.

5. V. Petrushko (deputy chairman, Lvov Province Soviet Executive Committee; candidate of economic sciences), "It is Still Difficult To Be Zakazchik," SDT, No. 4 (April 1968), p. 28.

6. Ibid., p. 30.

7. Ibid., p. 31.

8. A. Iagodzinskii, "Multiplying One's Forces," Izvestiia, December 13. 1965, p. 3.

9. Ibid. Needed, said the mayor, were rules that would permit the city to spend whatever money it could accumulate—in Soviet parlance, "free limits" for drafting and construction expenses.

10. According to Petrushko (p. 30), incentive fund-financed housing construction increased in value from 7 million rubles (province-wide) in 1965 to 14 million in 1968. The amount offered to local soviets (including province and district as well as city governments) rose from 1 million to 5 million rubles during the same years.

11. A. Iagodzinskii, "The Rights of the City's Master," Izvestiia, October 18, 1968, p. 3.

12. E. Grishaev, "One Master for Housing Construction," SDT, No. 5 (May 1961), p. 48.

13. Ibid., p. 48.

14. See SDT, No. 11 (November 1961), p. 77.

15. A. Tokarev (first secretary, Kuibishev Province Party Committee), "Party Organizations and Local Soviets," SDT, No. 8 (August 1966), p. 12.

16. G. Kisilinskii, "In the Interest of the Zakazchik," Izvestiia, June 9, 1965, p. 3.

17. Ibid.

18. A. Rosovskii, "Imaginary Economizing; Real Losses," Izvestiia, February 8, 1966, p. 3.

19. Quoted in A. Mikhailik, "Problems Demanding Solutions," SDT, No. 2 (August 1957), p. 75.

20. "The City Grows Faster," Izvestiia, June 5, 1965, p. 3.

21. RSFSR Zasedaniia (5th call; 7th session; December 19-20, 1962), p. 155.

22. Ibid., p. 177.

23. P. Novokshonov, "An Hour of City Life," Izvestiia, May 12, 1966, p. 3. Except where otherwise noted, the following account is based on this article. For a similar study of Khabarovsk, see "The Passengers Are Waiting," Pravda, December 16, 1965, p. 2.

24. I. Serikov, "Why Did They Write 800,000?" SDT, No. 9 (September 1966), p. 24. Tomsk officials pleaded guilty in SDT, No. 6 (June 1967), p. 73.

25. SDT, No. 1 (January 1960), p. 72.

26. V. Zorikhin (chairman, Arkhangelsk Soviet Executive Committee), "The Concerns of a Northern City," Izvestiia, July 8, 1966, p. 3.

27. A. Taff (architect, assistant professor, Institute for Engineering Construction), "From Plans to Construction," Pravda, August 19, 1969, p. 3.

28. I. Serikov, "When Comrades Disagree," SDT, No. 8 (August 1963), p. 80.

29. Ye. Kachalovskii, "Harmonious Development for the City," Izvestiia, August 27, 1969, p. 3.

30. A. Sokolov, "The Autonomy of the City," Izvestiia, November 3, 1968, p. 2.

31. Quoted in L. Lubian, "Seven Nannies in Zaporozhe," SDT, No. 10 (October 1962), p. 48.

32. See E. Grishaev, "New Department of the Ispolkom," SDT, No. 11 (November 1958), pp. 60-64.

33. V. Zorin, "A Second Step Is Needed," Izvestiia, May 10, 1962, p. 3.

CHAPTER 10

1. Statistics are cited in Cattell, Leningrad: A Case Study of Soviet Urban Government p. 144. He notes that the Leningrad city government "has been fortunate in having inherited all the pre-revolutionary housing that, until recently, constituted the bulk of housing in Leningrad." The Institute of Study and Law study is V. Chkhikvadze, I. Pavlov, and I. Azovkin, "Increasing the Role

of the Soviets Is an Immediate Task," SDT, No. 8 (August 1965), p. 15.

Compared to other cities, Moscow is well supplied with municipal services—100 percent of its housing has electricity, 98 percent has gas, 97 percent has running water and 93 percent has central heating. See Poliak, Biudzhet Moskvy, (Moscow: Izdatel'-stvo Ekonomeka, 1968) p. 173.

2. Personal interview.

3. For rebukes concerning sanitation see Bulletin-Moscow, No. 14 (July 1964), pp. 11-14; and No. 22 (November 1966), pp. 43-47. On winter housing, see No. 19 (October 1964), pp. 8-10. On retrieval of land, see No. 23 (December 1965), p. 17. On pollution, see No. 3 (February 1965), pp. 7-10; and No. 18 (September 1965), pp. 3-7.

4. See Cattell, "Local Government and Sovnarkhoz in the USSR," Soviet Studies XV, 4 (April 1964), pp. 437-38.

5. For Pegov's speech, see RSFSR Zasedaniia (5th call; 7th session; December 19-20, 1962), p. 64. The Krasnopresnenskii borough chairman, V. V. Fedorov, spoke to a city Party conference as recorded in Vechernaia Moskva, March 6, 1966, p. 3. Kruglova wrote "Your Time and Mine," Izvestiia, October 18, 1966, p. 4.

6. Cattell, "Leningrad: A Case Study of Soviet Local Government," p. 191.

7. On plans unfulfilled, see Bulletin-Moscow, No. 17 (September 1964), pp. 9-11, 16-20; No. 21 (November 1964), pp. 1-8; No. 1 (January 1966), pp. 3-13; and No. 22 (November 1966), p. 24. On cadre problems, see No. 23 (December 1965), p. 8; and No. 3 (February 1966), pp. 2-5.

8. M. Raman, "Features of a City," Izvestiia, April 28, 1966, p. 3.

9. For details of a land grant proceeding, see Bulletin-Moscow, No. 11 (June 1966), p. 24. On plans and drafts, see No. 5 (March 1966), pp. 8-11.

10. See speech by A. V. Dynkin, Vesiouznoe soveshchanie po gradostroitel'stvy, 7-10 iunia, 1960 (Moscow: Gosstroizdat, 1960), p. 297. Leningrad's chief architect, V. A. Kovol, expressed similar sentiments—Ibid., p. 269.

11. RSFSR Zasedaniia (5th call; 7th session December 19-20, 1962), p. 64.

12. Quoted in a Moscow Soviet resolution on the TEB in Bulletin-Moscow, No. 22 (November 1966), p. 34.

13. Sovetskii Souiz No. 3 (March 1967), p. 6.

14. Bulletin-Moscow, No. 22 (November 1966), p. 34.

15. USSR Zasedaniia (6th call; 3rd session; December 16-19, 1962), p. 130.

16. See speech by A. Ye. Biriukov (secretary, Moscow City Party Committee) in Zasedaniia Verkhovnogo Soveta RSFSR: stenograficheskii otchet (Meetings of the RSFSR Supreme Soviet: stenographic report) (hereafter abbreviated as RSFSR Zasedaniia) (6th call; 2nd session; December 1963), p. 64.

17. USSR Zasedaniia (6th call; 5th session; December 1964), pp. 93-94.

18. USSR Zasedaniia (6th call; 7th session; December 7-9, 1965), p. 115.

19. "The Talent of an Economist," Novyi mir, No. 1 (January 1967), as translated in CDSP, XIX, No. 13 (1967), p. 15.

20. The USSR decree is quoted in D. I. Bogorad, "On Limiting Growth of Large Cities and Developing Small Ones," Opyt proektirovaniia gorodov Ukrainy i Moldavii (Experience in planning cities in the Ukraine and Moldavia) (Kiev, 1965), p. 18. The RSFSR decree is quoted in Bulletin-Moscow, No. 19 (October 1966), p. 19. The Congress spoke in its Directives for the Five-year Plan. Final TEB approval is noted in Bulletin-Moscow, No. 22 (November 1966), p. 33.

21. Bulletin-Moscow, No. 22 (November 1966), p. 8.

22. Ibid., pp. 13-14.

23. Ibid., p. 29.

24. Bulletin-Moscow, No. 22 (November 1966), p. 24.

25. Plenum CC, June 24-29, 1959, pp. 617-18.

26. Svetlichnyi, "Soviet City Planning," p. 56.

27. I. Boltovskii (director, chief capital construction administration, Moscow City Soviet), "Single Zakazchik," Pravda, November 18, 1967, p. 2. According to Romanov, Leningrad authorities also had difficulty consolidating zakazchik power; see Izvestiia, December 17, 1966, p. 4.

28. See USSR Zasedaniia (5th call; 6th session; December 20-23, 1960), p. 160. Khrushchev's comment was brief, lacking either accusations or proposals for change: "Coordinated construction of residential districts plays a key role in city planning. Schools, kindergartens, stores and other cultural-everyday services should be completed when houses are. But, as a general rule, these lag behind housing construction" (Plenum CC, November 19-23, 1962, p. 41).

For 1962 speeches, see USSR Zasedaniia (6th call; 2nd session; December 10-13, 1962). Spokesmen were Moscow's chief architect, M. V. Posokhin; Leningrad ispolkom chairman V. V. Isaev; and Kiev Party first secretary V. I. Drozdenko. Before becoming chairman in 1962, Isaev served as deputy chairman (1961-62) and head of the chief construction administration (1955-61); in 1966 he became first deputy chairman of USSR Gosplan specializing in construction.

29. USSR Zasedaniia (6th call; 5th session; December 9-11, 1964), p. 138.

30. Ibid., p. 370.

31. Ibid., p. 105.

32. USSR Zasedaniia (6th call; 7th session; December 7-9, 1965), p. 116.

33. Izvestiia, December 17, 1967, p. 3.

34. USSR Zasedaniia (5th call; 6th session; December 20-23, 1960), p. 50.

35. RSFSR Zasedaniia (5th call; 7th session; December 19-20, 1962), p. 63.

36. Bulletin-Moscow, No. 22 (November 1966), p. 28.

CHAPTER 11

1. On the conception of a Soviet-military-industrial complex, see Vernon Aspaturian, "The Soviet Military Industrial Complex— Does It Exist?" Journal of International Affairs, Vol. XXVI, No. 1 (1972), pp. 1-28.

2. I am indebted to Professor Henry Morton for bringing this comparison to my attention.

3. L. Kantorovich, (chairman, Academy of Sciences Commission for Mathematical Economics and Operations Research), "The Service Sector and Science," Pravda, March 20, 1967, p. 2. L. Karlinskii and L. Pochivalov report that a selected sample of Muscovites spent up to 70 percent of their nonworking time on lines—"in stores, laundries, cafeterias, tailor shops, bus stops, etc." (See "Everyday Services and Price of time," Pravda, January 23, 1966, p. 2). Studies at several large factories in Leningrad showed that men spent more than 37 percent, and women more than 57 percent, of nonwork time on housework and on obtaining various consumer services (See Kruglova, "Your Time and Mine," Izvestiia, October 18, 1966, p. 4).

4. For relevant biographical data see Jerry F. Hough, "Soviet Urban Politics and Comparative Urban Theory," The Journal of Comparative Administration, IV, 3 (November 1972), p. 332, n. 12.

5. Richard M. Merelman, "On the Neo-Elitist Critique of Community Power," American Political Science Review, LXII, 2 (June 1968), 451.

6. Merelman's essay is as good an introduction as any to the community power literature. Floyd Hunter wrote Community Power Structure (Chapel Hill: University of North Carolina Press, 1953). Pluralist treatments include Robert Dahl's Who Governs? (New Haven: Yale University Press, 1961); and Nelson Polsby, Community Power and Political Theory (New Haven: Yale University Press, 1963). A book presenting the neo-elitist position is

Peter Bachrach and Morton S. Baratz, Power and Poverty: Theory and Practice (New York: Oxford University Press, 1970).

7. H. Gordon Skilling, "Interest Groups and Communist Politics: An Introduction," in Skilling and Franklyn Griffiths, eds., Interest Groups in Soviet Politics (Princeton: Princeton University Press, 1971), p. 17.

8. Andrew S. McFarland, Power and Leadership in Pluralist Systems (Stanford: Stanford University Press, 1969), pp. 88-89.

9. See Dahl, "A Critique of the Ruling Elite Model," American Political Science Review, 52, 2 (June 1958), pp. 463-71; and Polsby, Community Power and Political Theory, especially Chapters One and Four.

10. McFarland, Power and Leadership, p. 89.

11. William I. Connolly, "The Challenge to Pluralist Theory," in Connolly, ed., The Bias of Pluralism (New York: Atherton Press, 1969), pp. 18-19.

12. See Theodore J. Lowi, "American Business, Public Policy, Case-Studies and Political Theory," World Politics, XVI, 4 (July 1964), 690-91; and Lowi, "Making Democracy Safe for the World," in James N. Rosenau, ed., Domestic Sources of Foreign Policy (New York: The Free Press, 1967), p. 297.

13. Connolly, "The Challenge to Pluralist Theory," p. 13.

14. Jerry F. Hough, "The Soviet System: Petrification or Pluralism?" Problems of Communism, Vol. No. 2 (March/April 1972), p. 31.

15. On the politics of environmental reform, see David E. Powell, "The Social Costs of Modernization: Ecological Problems in the USSR," World Politics, XXIII, 4 (July 1971), 618-34. For an analysis attributing the decline and fall of the September 1965 economic reforms to the opposition of entrenched middle-level administrators as well as conservative Party ideologues, see Gertrude Schroeder, "Soviet Economic Reforms at an Impasse," Problems of Communism, XX, 4 (July/August 1971), 36-46.

16. For two recent surveys, see Alfred G. Meyer, "Theories of Convergence," in Chalmers Johnson, ed., Change in Communist Systems (Stanford: Stanford University Press, 1970), pp. 313-14; and John S. Nelson, "Theories of Convergence," Newsletter on the Comparative Study of Communism, 4, 2 (February 1971), 11-28. I am not entirely in agreement, however, with classifications employed in these articles—for example, Professor Meyer's placing in the same category of both W. W. Rostow and J. Kenneth Galbraith, two people who have very different notions as to where the two systems stand, and what's right or wrong with them.

17. See Isaac Deutscher, Russia in Transition (New York: Coward-McCann, 1957).

18. Zbigniew Brzezinski and Samuel P. Huntington, Political Power USA/USSR, p. 10.

19. For argumentation supporting my point about resurrected convergence theory, see William Taubman, "The Change to Change in Communist Systems: Modernization, Post-Modernization and Soviet Politics" (paper prepared for delivery at Annual Meeting of the American Political Science Association, Washington, D.C., September 5-9, 1972). Brzezinski's version may be found in Brzezinski, "The Soviet Political System: Transformation or Degeneration," Problems of Communism, XV, 1 (January/February 1966), pp. 1-15; and in Brzezinski, Between Two Ages: America's Role in the Technetronic Era (New York, Viking Press, 1970). Other articles in the same general mode include those by Chalmers Johnson, Richard Lowenthal, R. V. Burks, and Zvi Y. Gitelman, in Chalmers Johnson, ed., Change in Communist Systems.

20. See James Burnham, The Managerial Revolution (New York: John Day, 1941), especially Chapters 6, 7, and 14.

21. J. Kenneth Galbraith, The New Industrial State (New York: Signet, 1967), p. 397.

22. Robert L. Heilbroner, "Socialism and the Future," Commentary, 48, 9 (December 1969), 41-42.

23. Jeremy Azrael, "The Managers," in R. Barry Farrell, ed., Political Leadership in Eastern Europe and the Soviet Union (Chicago: Aldine, 1970), p. 247.

24. Jerry F. Hough, "The Soviet System: Petrification or Pluralism?" p. 38.

25. Daniel Bell, "The Corporation and Society in the 1970's," The Public Interest, 24 (Summer 1971), pp. 10-11, 21.

26. See Andrei Amalrik, Will the USSR Survive 1984? (New York: Harper and Row, 1970).

APPENDIXES
     1. This account draws on Sovetskoe finansovoe pravo (Moscow: Iuridicheskaia Literatura, 1961), especially pp. 104-106; and on Swearer, "Soviet Local Government in the USSR: Public Participation in a Totalitarian Society," (unpublished Ph.D. dissertation, Harvard University, 1960) and on B. Michael Frolic, "Decision Making in Soviet Cities," pp. 38-52. The process described is actually that of budget formulation, but since plan and budget are opposite sides of the same coin, and since both are prepared in similar ways, I follow Swearer's lead in referring to "the budget-plan process."
     2. Sovetskoe finansovoe pravo, p. 135.

This bibliography is a selective listing of sources consulted. In addition to those cited in footnotes in the text, it includes other particularly relevant and useful books and articles. Specific decrees and speeches cited in the text are not repeated individually in the bibliography; collections of statutes and speeches are listed in a separate section below.

SOVIET MATERIALS

Books and Monographs

Amalrik, Andrei. Will the USSR Survive 1984? New York: Harper and Row, 1970.

Azovkin, I. A. Oblastnoi (kraevoi) sovet deputatov trudiashchikhsia (The province [regional] soviet). Moscow: Iuridicheskaia Literatura, 1962.

_____. Organizatsiia raboty v ispolkome raionnogo soveta (Organization of work in the district soviet). Moscow: Iuridicheskaia Literatura, 1959.

Barabashev, G. V., and K. F. Sheremet. Sovetskoe stroitel'stvo (Soviet affairs). Moscow: Iuridicheskaia Literatura, 1965.

Bartyshev, B. I. "Kompetentsiia raionnogo soveta deputatov trudiashchikhsia na sovremennom etape" (The competence of district soviets at present stage). Unpublished Kandidat dissertation, Moscow State University, 1965.

Gabrichidze, B. N. Gorodskie sovety deputatov trudiashchikhsia (City soviets). Moscow: Iuridicheskaia Literatura, 1968.

Iampol'skaia, Ts. A., A. V. Luzhin, and A. S. Pribluda, eds. Pravovye voprosy organizatsii i deiatel'nosti sovnarkhozov (Legal problems of the organization and activities of sovnarkhozy). Moscow: Izdatel'stvo Akademii Nauk SSSR, 1961.

Karapetian, L., and V. Razin. Sovety obshchenarodnogo gosudarstva (Soviets of the all-peoples' state). Moscow: Izdatel'stvo Politicheskoi Literatury, 1964.

Kazarinova, V. I., and V. I. Pavlichenkov. Magnitogorsk. Moscow: Izdatel'stvo Literatury po Stroitel'stvu, Arkhitekture i Stroitel'nym Materialam, 1961.

Kozlov, Iu. M., ed. Sovershenstvovanie demokraticheskikh printsipov v sovetskom gosudarstvennom upravlenii (Perfecting democratic principles in Soviet state administration). Moscow: Izdatel'stvo Moskovskogo Universiteta, 1966.

_____, ed. Sovetskoe administrativnoe pravo (Soviet administrative law). Moscow: Iuridicheskaia Literatura, 1964.

Mamutov, V. K. Kompetentsiia gosudarstvennykh organov v reshenii khoziastvennykh voprosov (The competence of state organs in the solution of economic problems). Moscow: Iuridicheskaia Literatura, 1964.

Marchuk, V. M. "Osnovnye napravlieniia sovershenstvovaniia apparata gosudarstvennogo upravleniia v sovermennon usloviakh" (Basic directions of the perfecting of the state administrative apparatus under present conditions). Unpublished Kandidat dissertation, Academy of Sciences of the Ukrainian SSR, 1965.

Mestnye sovety na sovremennom etape (Local soviets at the present stage). Moscow: Nauka, 1965.

Nizhechek, V. I. "Sochetanie gosudarstvennykh i obshchestvennykh nachal v organizatsii i deiatel'nosti mestnykh sovetov deputatov trudiashchikhsia" (The combination of state and non-state principles in the organization and activities of local soviets). Unpublished Kandidat dissertation, Irkutsk State University, 1963.

Osnovy sovetskogo gradostroitel'stva (Foundations of Soviet urban development). 3 vols. Moscow: Stroiizdat, 1966-67.

Pertsik, V. A. Problemy mestnogo samoupravleniia v SSSR (Problems of local self-government in the USSR). Vol. XXXII, No. 6. Juridical Series, Trudy Irkutskogo gosudarstvennogo universiteta (Works of Irkutsk State University). Irkutsk, 1963.

Poliak, G. B. Budzet Moskvy (Moscow's budget). Moscow: Izdatel'stvo Ekonomika, 1968.

Razin, V. I., ed. Stanovlenie kommunisticheskogo samoupravleniia (Coming of Communist self-government). Moscow: Izdatel'stvo Moskovskogo Universiteta, 1965.

Safarov, R. A. Raionnye sovety deputatov trudiashchikhsia v gorodakh (Borough soviets in cities). Moscow: Gosiurizdat, 1961.

Shirkevich, N. Mestnye biudzhety SSSR (USSR local budgets). Moscow: Finansy, 1965.

Sorok let sovetskogo prava (Forty years of Soviet law). Vol. II. Leningrad, 1957.

Sovetskoe finansovoe pravo (Soviet financial law). Moscow: Iuridicheskaia Literatura, 1961.

Tikhomirov, Iu. A. Mestnye sovety i sovnarkhozy (Local soviets and sovnarkhozy). Moscow: Gosiurizdat, 1959.

_____. Sovety i razvitie gosudarstvennogo upravleniia v period razvernutogo stroitel'stva kommunizma (Soviets and the development of state administration in the period of the all-round construction of Communism). Moscow: Iuridicheskaia Literatura, 1963.

Trotsky, L. D. The Revolution Betrayed. New York: Pioneer Publishers, 1945.

Voprosy partiinogo stroitel'stva (Problems of Party work). 3 vols. Leningrad: Lenizdat, 1960-65.

Documents, Statutes, Resolutions,
Speeches, and Reports

Administrativnye shtrafy: sbornik normativnykh aktov (Administrative fines: Collected legislation). Iuridicheskaia Literatura, 1965.

Akademiia Nauk Ukrainskoi SSR. 570 voprosov i otvetov po sovetskomu zakonodatel'stvu (570 questions and answers on Soviet legislation). Kiev: "Naukova dumka," 1965.

Andreevskii, I. N., ed. Spravochnik po zakonodatel'stvu dlia rabotnikov zhilishchno-kommunal'nogo khoziastva (Handbook on legislation for workers in housing municipal services). Moscow: Stroizdat, 1964.

Bor'ba KPSS za zavershenie stroitel'stva sotsializma (The struggle of the CPSU for the completion of the building of socialism). Moscow: Gospolitizdat, 1961.

Deputaty Soveta Soiuza i Soveta Natsional'nostei Verkhovnogo Soveta SSSR (Deputies of the Council of the Union and the Council of Nationalities of the USSR Supreme Soviet). Moscow, 1959.

Iuridicheskii spravochnik deputata mestnogo soveta (Legal handbook for the local soviet deputy). 2nd ed., Moscow: Izdatel'stvo Moskovskogo Universiteta, 1962.

Iuridicheskii spravochnik khoziaistvennika (Legal handbook for the manager). Moscow: Izdatel'stvo Moskovskogo Universiteta, 1963.

Khazikov, A. G., ed. Sbornik normativnykh aktov po sovetskomu administrativnomu pravu (Collected administrative law statutes). Moscow: Vysshaia shkola, 1964.

Konstitutsiia SSSR (The USSR Constitution). Moscow: "Izvestiia," 1965.

KPSS v resoliutskiakh i resheniakh s"ezdov, konferentsii i plenumov TsK (The CPSU in resolutions and decisions of congresses, conferences and plenums of the Central Committee). Moscow: Politizdat, 1960.

Moscow: General Plan for the Reconstruction of the City. Moscow: Union of Soviet Architects, 1935.

Narodnoe khoziastvo SSSR v 1964 (The national economy of the USSR in 1964). Moscow, 1965.

Pamiatka deputatov mestnogo soveta deputatov trudiashchikhsia Krasnodarskogo kraia (Rules for the local soviet deputy in Krasnodarsk Region). Krasnodar, 1965.

Plenum Tsentral'nogo Komiteta Kommunisticheskoi Partii Sovetskogo Soiuza, 24-29 iiunia, 1959: stenograficheskii otchet. (Plenum

of the Central Committee of the Communist Party of the Soviet
Union, June 24-29, 1959, stenographic report). Moscow:
Izdatel'stvo Politicheskoi Literatury, 1959.

Plenum Tsentral'nogo Komiteta Kommunisticheskoi Partii Sovetskogo
Soiuza, 19-23 noiabria, 1962: stenograficheskii otchet (Plenum
of the Central Committee of the Communist Party of the Soviet
Union, November 19-23, 1962: stenographic report). Moscow:
Izdatel'stvo Politicheskoi Literatury, 1963.

Programme of the Communist Party of the Soviet Union. Moscow:
Foreign Languages Publishing House, 1961.

Rozantsev, S. Sto otvetov na voprosy po zhilishchnomu zakonodatel'stvu
(One hundred answers to questions on housing legislation).
Moscow: Profizdat, 1965.

Sbornik obiazatel'nykh postanovlenii i reshenii ispol'nitel'nogo
komiteta Moskovskogo gorodskogo soveta (Collected Obligatory
Decrees and Decisions of the Moscow City Soviet). Moscow:
Moskovskii Rabochii, 1941.

Sostav deputatov mestnykh sovetov deputatov trudiashchikhsia
izbrannykh v marte 1965 (The composition of deputies of local
soviets elected in March, 1965). Moscow: Izdatel'stvo Izvestiia,
1965.

Spravochnik narodnogo kontrolera (Handbook for the people's con-
troller). Moscow: Izdatel'stvo Politicheskoi Literatury, 1964.

Spravochnik profsoiuznogo rabotnika (Handbook for the trade union
worker). Moscow: Profizdat, 1965.

SSSR: Administrativno-territorial'noe delenie soiuznykh respublik,
1965 (Administrative-Territorial divisions of the union-
republics, 1965). Moscow, 1965.

Uchastie obshchestvennosti v rabote mestnykh sovetov (Participation
by the public in the work of local soviets). Irkutsk, 1964.

Ustav Kommunisticheskoi Partii Sovetskogo Soiuza (Rules of the
Communist Party of the Soviet Union). Moscow: Politizdat,
1965.

Vsesoiuznoe soveshchanie po gradostroitel'stvy, 7-10, iunia, 1960:
sokrashchennyi otchet (All-Union conference on urban development, June 7-10, 1960: Condensed record). Moscow:
Gostroizdat, 1960.

Zasedaniia Verkhovnogo Soveta RSFSR, piatogo sozyva, sed'maia
sessia (19-20 dekabria, 1962): stenograficheskii otchet (Sessions
of the RSFSR Supreme Soviet, 5th call, 7th session, December
19-20, 1962: Stenographic record). Moscow, 1963.

Zasedaniia Verkhovnogo Soveta RSFSR, shestogo sozyva, vtoraia
sessiia (17-19 dekabria, 1963): stenograficheskii otchet (Sessions
of the RSFSR Supreme Soviet, 6th call, 2nd session, December
17-19, 1963: Stenographic record). Moscow, 1964.

Zasedaniia Verkhovnogo Soveta SSSR, chetvertogo sozyva, chetvertaia
sessiia (26-29, dekabria, 1955): stenograficheskii otchet
(Sessions of the USSR Supreme Soviet, 4th call, 4th session,
December 26-29, 1955: Stenographic record). Moscow, 1956.

Zasedaniia Verkhovnogo Soveta SSSR, chetvertogo sozyva, pervaia
sessia, (20-27 aprelia, 1954): stenograficheskii otchet (Sessions
of the USSR Supreme Soviet, 4th call, 1st session, April 20-27,
1954: Stenographic record). Moscow, 1954.

Zasedaniia Verkhovnogo Soveta SSSR, shestogo sozyva, piataia sessiia
(9-11 dekabria, 1964): stenograficheskii otchet (USSR Supreme
Soviet, 6th call, 5th session, December 9-11, 1964). Moscow,
1965.

Zasedaniia Verkhovnogo Soveta SSSR, shestogo sozyva, tretaia sessia
(16-19 dekabria, 1963): stenograficheskii otchet (USSR Supreme
Soviet, 6th call, 3rd session, December 16-19, 1963). Moscow,
1964.

Zasedaniia Verkhnovnogo Soveta SSSR, shestogo sozyva, vtoraia sessiia
(10-13 dekabria, 1962): stenograficheskii otchet (USSR Supreme
Soviet, 6th call, 2nd session, December 10-13, 1962). Moscow,
1963.

Zasedaniia Verkhovnogo Soveta SSSR, shestogo sozyva, sed'maia
sessiia 7-9 dekabria, 1965): stenograficheskii otchet (USSR
Supreme Soviet, 6th call, 7th session, December 7-9, 1965).
Moscow, 1966.

Zhilishchno-bytovye voprosy: sbornik rukovodiashchikh materialov
    (Problems of housing and everyday services: Collected rulings).
    Moscow: Profizdat, 1964.

Articles

Acharkan, V. A. "Legal Regulations on the Use of Funds for Social-
    Cultural Measures and Housing Construction." Sovetskoe
    gosudarstvo i pravo (hereafter, SGP), No. 4 (April 1967), pp.
    28-47.

Alekseev, T. Procedures for Construction and Acceptance of Apart-
    ment Houses and Other Buildings," Sovety deputatov trudiashchi-
    khsia (hereafter SDT), No. 1 (January 1959), pp. 94-96.

Antonov, V., and E. Grishaev. "Who Is the Master in Krivoi Rog?"
    SDT, No. 4 (April 1960), pp. 75-80.

Arutunian, I. "Both All-Union and Republic. . . ." SDT, No. 1
    (January 1967), pp. 68-74.

Azovkin, I. "The Development of the Material-Financial Base and
    of the Competence of Local Soviets," Mestnye sovety na
    sovremennom etape (Local soviets at the present stage).
    Moscow: Nauka, 1965.

_____. "On the Material Base of Local Soviets," SDT, No. 9
    (September 1965), pp. 58-63.

Barabashev, G. V. "The Role and Situation of Municipal Organs in
    the States Ruled by Monopolies," SGP, No. 7 (July 1965), pp.
    55-64.

Barabashev, G. V., K. F. Sheremet, and P. Titov. "The Role of the
    Soviets in the Development of the Soviet Economy," SDT, No. 12
    (December 1965), pp. 7-20.

Baranov, N. "On Theories of Dynamic Urban Development,"
    Arkhitektura SSSR, No. 3 (March 1967), pp. 29-35.

Bechvaia, T. "Who Is the Master of Gagra?" SDT, No. 3 (March
    1967), pp. 33-36.

Birman, A. "The Talent of an Economist," Novyi mir, No. 1 (January 1967), pp. 167-89.

Bogorad, D. I. "On Limiting the Growth of Large Cities and Developing Small Ones," Opyt proektirovaniia gorodov Ukrainy i Moldavii (Experience in planning cities in the Ukraine and Moldavia). Kiev, 1965.

Boltovskii, I. "Single Zakazchik," Pravda, November 18, 1967, p. 2.

Bosenko, I. "In One Pair of Hands," Izvestiia, February 1, 1970, p. 3.

Burkova, Inessa. "Kuzma," Literaturnaia Rossiia, May 6, 1966, pp. 16-17.

"Caring about the Plan, Caring about People," Izvestiia, April 4, 1961, p. 1.

Chivilikhin, Vladimir. "How Is Your Breathing City Dweller?" Literaturnaia gazeta, August 9, 1967, p. 10.

Chkhikvadze, V., I. Pavlov, and I. Azovkin. "Increasing the Role of Soviets Is an Immediate Task," SDT, No. 8 (August 1965), pp. 9-18.

Churakov, N. "The Assertion of Power," SDT, No. 12 (December 1967), pp. 81-85.

"The City Grows Faster," Izvestiia, June 5, 1965, p. 3.

Davydchenkov, V., and Iu. Feofanov. "The City and its Soviet," Izvestiia, January 26, 1961, p. 3.

Dolenko, A. "The Case of the Factory Path," Izvestiia, May 10, 1962, p. 3.

Drozdov, I. "A City Without a Master," Izvestiia, October 20, 1960, p. 3.

Fesenko, A. "The Chief Architect," SDT, No. 8 (August 1965), pp. 75-79.

Feofanov, I., and Morozov, S. "Smiles and Grimaces." Izvestiia, July 19, 1961, p. 3.

Filatov, L. "Province Soviet Executive Committees and the Sovnarkhoz," SDT, No. 1 (January 1958), pp. 27-32.

Gabrichidze, B., and M. Shafir. "Soviet and Enterprise," Izvestiia, October 16, 1966, p. 3.

Gin'ko, V. "The Concern of Small Cities," Izvestiia, March 15, 1966, p. 3.

Golovin, A. "The Statute May Be New, but What about the Conditions?" SDT, No. 12 (December 1967), pp. 29-33.

"Goodbye to the Last Barracks," Vecherniaia Moskva, March 18, 1966, p. 2.

Grishaev, E. "New Department of the Ispolkom," SDT, No. 11 (November 1958), pp. 60-64.

Iagodzinskii, A. "Multiplying One's Forces," Izvestiia, December 13, 1965, p. 3.

_____. "The Rights of the City's Master," Izvestiia, October 18, 1968, p. 3.

Iakovlev, I. "Winter Takes Its Toll," Izvestiia, February 16, 1964, p. 3.

Ignat'ev, N. "The Public Table of the City," SDT, No. 5 (May 1967), pp. 41-45.

Isliukov, S. "The Large Problems of Small Cities," SDT, No. 6 (June 1966), pp. 21-25.

Ivakin, A. "The City Soviet and the Agencies," Izvestiia, June 9, 1965, p. 3.

Kachalovskii, E. "Harmonious Development for the City," Izvestiia, August 27, 1969, p. 3.

Kantorovich, L. "The Service Sector and Science." Pravda, March 20, 1967, p. 2.

Kardanol'tsev, A., and A. Rozhdestvenskii. "Here There Will be a Master," Izvestiia, June 28, 1961, p. 3.

Karlinskii, L., and L. Pochivalov. "Everyday Services and the Price of Time," Pravda, January 23, 1966, p. 2.

Khripko, L. "The Trust and the City," SDT, No. 3 (March 1966), pp. 31-34.

Kisilinskii, G. "In the Interest of the Zakazchik," Izvestiia, June 9, 1965, p. 3.

Komkov, N. "Some Problems in Developing the Communal Economy," SDT, No. 6 (December 1957), pp. 21-26.

Kruglova, Z. "Your Time and Mine," Izvestiia, October 18, 1966, p. 4.

Kucherenko, V. "Several Questions of Soviet Urban Development," Pravda, June 1, 1960, pp. 2-3.

Lagunov, K. "A Town Is Being Built in the Taiga," Pravda, October 22, 1969.

Lazarev, B. M. "On the Delegation of Power in the Sphere of State Administration," SGP, No. 10 (October 1965), pp. 27-35.

Levishchev, I. "The City of District Subordination," SDT, No. 3 (March 1958), pp. 74-77.

Liberman, Ye. "The Queue: Its Anamnesis, Diagnosis, Therapy," Literaturnaia gazeta, March 10, 1968, p. 10.

Lubian, L. "Seven Nannies in Zaporozhe," SDT, No. 10 (October 1964), pp. 46-48.

Mamutov, V. K. "Responsibility of Higher Organs in Economic-Administrative Relations," SGP, No. 3 (March 1966), pp. 44-52.

Martynov, K. "Experience with the New System of Planning and Economic Incentives," SGP, No. 5 (May 1967), pp. 98-103.

Mikhailik, A. "Problems Demanding Solutions," SDT, No. 2 (August 1957), pp. 75-77.

Mkrtchian, M. "Methodological Questions of the Geographic Distribution of Productive Forces," Planovoe khoziaistvo, No. 12 (December 1969), pp. 36-45.

Mostovoi, P. "City and Factory," Izvestiia, July 7, 1965, p. 3.

Munarev, P. "Must a City Be Born in Torment?" SDT, No. 1
(January 1967), pp. 33-34.

Murzin, A. "Letters from Western Siberia," Pravda, March 8, 1970,
p. 2.

Negri, V. "If You Cannot Do It, Do Not Promise To; If You Promise,
Do It." Izvestiia, May 30, 1968, p. 3.

Novokshonov, P. "An Hour of City Life," Izvestiia, May 12, 1966,
p. 3.

"On the Preliminary Results of the 1970 All-Union Population Census,"
Pravda, April 19, 1970, pp. 1-2.

Ozerskii, A. "In a Young City," SDT, No. 4 (October 1957), pp.
79-82.

Pantiushenko, G., and E. Grishaev. "The City Soviet," SDT, No. 5
(May 1958), pp. 39-55.

Parfenov, V. "How Much Does a Liter of Water Cost?" Pravda,
May 21, 1966, p. 4.

Perevedentsev, V. "The Future of the Small City," Literaturnaia
gazeta, January 17, 1968, p. 11.

_____. "What Kind of City is Advantageous?" Literaturnaia
gazeta, September 20, 1967, p. 11.

Petrov, G. "On the Form and Content of New Laws," SDT, No.6
(June 1967), pp. 84-86.

Petrov, P., and I. Ivanov. "The New Statutes on the Socialist State
Production Enterprise," SGP, No. 1 (January 1966), pp. 17-25.

Petrushko, V. "It Is Still Difficult to Be Zakazchik." SDT, No. 4
(August 1968), pp. 28-32.

Polushin, I. "Your City is Not Municipal," Izvestiia, February 12,
1960, p. 4.

Protozanov, A. "Temporary Building or Permanent Apartment House?" Izvestiia, July 13, 1967, p. 3.

Raman, M. "Features of a City," Izvestiia, April 28, 1966, p. 3.

Rosovskii, A. "Imaginary Economizing; Real Losses," Izvestiia, February 8, 1966, p. 3.

Rozhkov, A. "On City Government," SDT, No. 7 (July 1968), pp. 74-77.

Rumiantsev, V. "Why Must They Supplant?" SDT, No. 11 (November 1965), pp. 63-65.

Sabaneev, S., and G. Konovalov. "Hand in Hand," Izvestiia, May 17, 1967, p. 3.

Shcherinov, N. "Put the City Economy into One Pair of Hands," SDT, No. 6 (June 1961), pp. 69-71.

Seliunin, V. "Our Daily Work," Moskva, No. 7 (July 1967), pp. 173-86.

Selivanov, A. and D. Ustimenko. "Important Tasks of the Executive Committee of the District Soviets," Biulleten' Ispolnitel'nogo Komiteta Moskovskogo Gorodskogo Soveta Deputatov Trudia-shchikhsia, No. 4 (February 1966), pp. 18-23.

Serikov, I. "Attention—A City Is Being Born," SDT, No. 9 (September 1965), pp. 38-42.

_____. "The Just Cause of the Metallurgists," SDT, No. 10 (October 1965), pp. 38-42.

_____. "When Comrades Disagree," SDT, No. 8 (August 1963), pp. 77-80.

_____. "Why Did They Write 800,000?" SDT, No. 9 (September 1966), pp. 22-24.

Shumskii, S., and N. Shchetini. "Essential Questions of City Planning," SDT, No. 9 (September 1960), pp. 19-25.

Sokolov, A. "The Autonomy of the City," Izvestiia, November 3, 1968, p. 3.

Sokol'ski, M. "Against Departmental Divisions," SDT, No. 9 (September 1966), pp. 29-34.

Sryvtsev, A. "Problems of Construction in a Big City," SDT, No. 10 (October 1959), p. 61-65.

Svetlichnyi, B. "Long Life for Apartment Houses," SDT, No. 12 (December 1967), pp. 25-29.

_____. "Man and the City," Oktiabr', No. 1 (January 1964), pp. 163-75.

_____. "Questions on the Long-term Development of Cities," Voprosy ekonomiki, No. 3 (March 1962), pp. 58-69.

_____. "Reflections on the Fate of Cities," Arkhitektura SSSR, No. 4 (April 1967), pp. 27-36.

_____. "Soviet City Planning at the Present Stage," Voprosy ekonomiki, No. 7 (July 1960), pp. 52-59.

_____. "Urban Development and City Planning," Arkhitektura SSSR, No. 3 (March 1966), pp. 28-32.

_____. "The City Awaits a Reply," Oktiabr', No. 10 (October 1966), pp. 157-69.

Taff, A. "From Plans to Construction," Pravda, August 19, 1969, p. 3.

"The Passengers Are Waiting," Pravda, December 16, 1965, p. 2.

"The Soviet Is Master of the City," Izvestiia, September 15, 1961, p. 1.

Tikhomirov, Iu. A. "The Development of the Democratic Bases of the Organization and Activities of Local Soviet Organs," Mestnye sovety na sovremennom etape. Moscow: Nauka, 1965.

Titov, I. "Cities Rise in the Taiga," Pravda, January 8, 1968, p. 3.

Tkach, Z. A. "Applying the Statute on the Socialist State Production Enterprise," SGP, No. 1 (January 1967), pp. 88-97.

Tokarev, A. "Party Organs and Local Soviets," SDT, No. 8 (August 1966), pp. 8-14.

Torskii, G. "Economic Calculations and Health Services." SDT,
No. 8 (August 1968), pp. 31-35.

Trubnikov, S. "Consumer Services and the Problem of Personnel,"
Planovoe khoziaistvo, No. 5 (May 1968), pp. 22-23.

Tutkarin, B. "Local Interest," Pravda, May 8, 1968, p. 3.

Valentei, D., and B. Khorev. "The Problems of the Cities," Ekonomicheskaia gazeta, No. 29 (July 1967), pp. 18-19.

Vershinin, M. "Protect Housing—The National Property," SDT, No. 7
(July 1961), pp. 14-18.

Vorotnikov, V. "Local Soviet and Enterprise," Izvestiia, August 1,
1968, p. 3.

"What Should the Statutes on Local Soviets Say?" SDT, No. 8 (August
1966), pp. 43-49.

Zorikhin, V. "The Concerns of a Northern City," Izvestiia, July 8,
1966, p. 3.

Zorin, V. "A Second Step Is Needed." Izvestiia, May 10, 1962, p. 3.

NON-SOVIET MATERIALS

Books and Monographs

Allison, Graham, T. Essence of Decision: Conceptual Models and
the Cuban Missile Crisis. Boston: Little, Brown, 1970.

Almond, Gabriel A., and G. Bingham Powell, Jr. Comparative Politics:
A Developmental Approach. Boston: Little, Brown, 1966.

Altshuler, Alan. The City Planning Process. Ithaca, N.Y.: Cornell
University Press, 1965.

Armstrong, John A. The Soviet Bureaucratic Elite. New York:
Frederick A. Praeger, 1959.

Azrael, Jeremy. Managerial Power and Soviet Politics. Cambridge,
Mass.: Harvard University Press, 1966.

Bachrach, Peter, and Morton S. Baratz. Power and Poverty: Theory and Practice. New York: Oxford University Press, 1970.

Banfield, Edward C. Political Influence. New York: The Free Press, 1961.

_____. The Unheavenly City: The Nature and Future of Our Urban Crisis. Boston: Little, Brown, 1970.

Banfield, Edward C., and James Q. Wilson. City Politics. New York: Random House (Vintage Books), 1966.

Barghoorn, Frederick C. Politics in the USSR. Boston: Little, Brown, 1966.

Berliner, Joseph. Factory and Manager in the USSR. Cambridge, Mass.: Harvard University Press, 1957.

Berman, Harold J., and John B. Quigley, Jr., eds. Basic Laws on the Structure of the Soviet State. Cambridge, Mass.: Harvard University Press, 1969.

Birnbaum, Norman. The Crisis of Industrial Society. New York: Oxford University Press, 1969.

Braybrooke, David and Charles E. Lindblom. A Strategy of Decision. Glencoe, Ill.: The Free Press of Glencoe, 1963.

Brzezinski, Zbigniew. Between Two Ages: America's Role in the Technotronic Era. New York: Viking Press, 1970.

Brzezinski, Zbigniew K., and Samuel P. Huntington. Political Power: USA/USSR. New York: Viking Press, 1963.

Cattell, David T. Leningrad: A Case Study of Soviet Urban Government. New York, Frederick A. Praeger, 1968.

Connolly, William I., ed. The Bias of Pluralism. New York: Atherton Press, 1969.

Churchward, L. G. Contemporary Soviet Government. New York: American Elsevier, 1968.

Crozier, Michel. The Bureaucratic Phenomenon. Chicago: University of Chicago Press, 1964.

Cyert, Richard M., and James G. March. A Behavioral Theory of the Firm. Englewood Cliffs, N. J.: Prentice-Hall, 1963.

Dahl, Robert A. Who Governs? New Haven: Yale University Press, 1961.

Deutscher, Isaac. Russia in Transition. New York: Coward-McCann, 1957.

Djilas, Milovan. The New Class. New York: Frederick A. Praeger, 1957.

Downs, Anthony. Inside Bureaucracy. Boston: Little, Brown, 1967.

Etzioni, Amitai. The Active Society. New York: The Free Press, 1968.

_____, ed. Complex Organizations. New York: Holt, Rinehart and Winston, 1961.

Fainsod, Merle. How Russia Is Ruled. Cambridge, Mass.: Harvard University Press, 1953. Also revised edition, 1963.

_____. Smolensk under Soviet Rule. Cambridge, Mass.: Harvard University Press, 1958.

Farrell, R. Barry, ed. Political Leadership in Eastern Europe and the Soviet Union. Chicago: Aldine, 1970.

Fisher, Jack C., ed. City and Regional Planning in Poland. Ithaca, N.Y.: Cornell University Press, 1966.

Fleron, Frederic J., Jr. Communism and the Social Sciences: Essays on Methodology and Empirical Theory. Chicago: Rand McNally, 1969.

Friedrich, Carl J., and Zbigniew K. Brzezinski. Totalitarian Dictatorship and Autocracy. 2nd ed. New York: Frederick A. Praeger, 1965.

Galbraith, J. K. The Affluent Society. Boston: Houghton Mifflin, 1957.

_____. The New Industrial State. New York: Signet Books, 1967.

Goldman, Marshall I. The Spoils of Progress: Environmental Pollution in the Soviet Union. Cambridge, Mass.: M.I.T. Press, 1972.

Hazard, John N. The Soviet System of Government. 4th ed. Chicago: University of Chicago Press, 1968.

Hirschman, Albert O. The Strategy of Economic Development. New Haven: Yale University Press, 1958.

Hough, Jerry F. The Soviet Prefects. Cambridge: Harvard University Press, 1969.

_____. "The Role of Local Party Organs in Soviet Industrial Decision-Making." Unpublished Ph.D. dissertation, Harvard University, 1961.

Hunter, Floyd. Community Power Structure. Chapel Hill: University of North Carolina Press, 1953.

Huntington, Samuel P., and Clement H. Moore, eds. Authoritarian Politics in Modern Society. New York: Basic Books, 1970.

Johnson, Chalmers, ed. Change in Communist Systems. Stanford: Stanford University Press, 1970.

Kanet, Roger E., ed. The Behavioral Revolution and Communist Studies. New York: The Free Press, 1971.

Kaufman, Herbert. Politics of State and Local Government. Englewood Cliffs, N.J.: Prentice-Hall, 1963.

LaPalombara, Joseph, ed. Bureaucracy and Political Development. Princeton: Princeton University Press, 1963.

Latham, Earl. The Group Basis of Politics. Ithaca, N.Y.: Cornell University Press, 1952.

Lindblom, Charles E. The Intelligence of Democracy. New York: The Free Press, 1965.

Lowi, Theodore J. The End of Liberalism: Ideology, Policy and the Crisis of Public Authority. New York: W. W. Norton, 1969.

March, James G., ed. Handbook of Organizations. Chicago: Rand McNally, 1965.

March, James G. and Herbert A. Simon. Organizations. New York: John Wiley, 1958.

Marcuse, Herbert, Barrington Moore Jr., and Robert Paul Wolff.
A Critique of Pure Tolerance. Boston: Beacon Press, 1965.

Mason, Edward S., ed. The Corporation in Modern Society. Cambridge, Mass.: Harvard University Press, 1959.

McFarland, Andrew. Power and Leadership in Pluralist Systems.
Stanford: Stanford University Press, 1970.

Meyer, Alfred G. The Soviet Political System: An Interpretation.
New York: Random House, 1965.

Nigro, Felix A. Modern Public Administration. 2nd edition. New
York: Harper and Row, 1970.

Osborn, Robert J. "Public Participation in Soviet City Government:
The Vision of the Future in the Light of Current Problems of
Urban Organization." Unpublished Ph.D. dissertation, Columbia
University, 1962.

_____. Soviet Social Policies: Welfare, Equality and Community.
Homewood, Ill.: Dorsey Press, 1970.

Parkins, M. F. City Planning in Soviet Russia. Chicago: University
of Chicago Press, 1953.

Polsby, Nelson. Community Power and Political Theory. New Haven:
Yale University Press, 1963.

Prominent Personalities in the USSR—1968. Metuchen, N.J.: The
Scarecrow Press, 1968.

Rabinovitz, Francine. City Politics and Planning. New York:
Atherton Press, 1969.

Saikowskii, Charlotte, and Leo Gruliow, eds. Current Soviet Policies
IV: The Documentary Record of the 22nd Congress of the
Communist Party of the Soviet Union. New York: Columbia
University Press, 1962.

Sayre, Wallace S., and Herbert Kaufman. Governing New York City.
New York: Russell Sage Foundation, 1960.

Scott, Mel. American City Planning Since 1890. Berkeley: University
of California Press, 1969.

Simon, E. D., Lady Simon, W. A., Robson and J. Jewke. Moscow in the Making. London: Longmans, Green, 1937.

Simon, Herbert A., Donald W. Smithburg, and Victor A. Thompson. Public Administration. New York: Alfred A. Knopf, 1950.

Stewart, Philip D. Political Power in the Soviet Union: A Study of Decision-Making in Stalingrad. New York: Bobbs-Merrill, 1968.

Swearer, Howard, R. "Local Government in the USSR: Public Participation in a Totalitarian Society." Unpublished Ph.D. dissertation, Harvard University, 1960.

Taubman, William. The View from Lenin Hills. New York: Coward-McCann, 1967.

Truman, David B. The Governmental Process. New York: Alfred A. Knopf, 1951.

Tullock, Gordon. The Politics of Bureaucracy. Washington, D.C.: Public Affairs Press, 1965.

United States Department of State. Directory of Soviet Officials— Vol. I: USSR and RSFSR; Vol. II: Union Republics. Washington: Government Printing Office, 1966.

Who's Who in the USSR—1965/1966. Montreal: Intercontinental Book and Publishing Company, 1966.

Wildavsky, Aaron. The Politics of the Budgetary Process. Boston: Little, Brown, 1964.

Articles

Aspaturian, Vernon. "The Soviet Military-Industrial Complex—Does it Exist?" Journal of International Affairs, 26, 1 (1972), pp. 1-28.

Black, Cyril E. "Soviet Society: A Comparative View." Prospects for Soviet Society. Edited by Allen Kassoff. New York: Frederick A. Praeger, 1968.

Bell, Daniel. "The Corporation and Society in the 1970's," The Public Interest, No. 24 (Summer 1971), pp. 5-32.

Brzezinski, Zbigniew K. "The Soviet Political System: Transformation or Degeneration," Problems of Communism, XV, 1 (January/February, 1966), 1-15.

Cattell, David T. "Leningrad: A Case Study of Soviet Local Government," Western Political Quarterly, XVII, 2 (June 1964), 188-99.

_____. "Local Government and the Sovnarkhoz in the USSR, 1957-1962," Soviet Studies, XV, 4 (April 1964), 430-42.

Churchward, L. G. "Soviet Local Government Today," Soviet Studies, XVII, 4 (April 1966), 431-52.

Dahl, Robert A. "A Critique of the Ruling Elite Model," American Political Science Review, LII, 2 (June 1958), 463-71.

Dyckman, John W. "The Scientific World of the City Planners," The American Behavioral Scientist, VI, 6 (February 1963), 46-50.

Fesler, James W. "Approaches to the Understanding of Decentralization," The Journal of Politics, XXVII, 3 (August 1965), 536-65.

Frolic, B. Michael. "Decision Making in Soviet Cities," American Political Science Review, LXVI, 1 (March 1972), 38-52.

_____. The Soviet Study of Soviet Cities," Journal of Politics, 32, 3 (August 1970), 675-95.

"Governmental Decision-Making," Public Administration Review, XXIV, 3 (September 1964), 153-65.

Grossman, Gregory. "Economic Reforms: A Balance Sheet," Problems of Communism, XV, 6 (November/December 1966), 43-61.

Heilbroner, Robert L. "Socialism and the Future," Commentary 48, 9 (December 1969), 35-45.

Hough, Jerry F. "Soviet Urban Politics and Comparative Urban Theory," The Journal of Comparative Administration, IV, 3 (November 1972), 311-34.

_____. "The Soviet Concept of the Relationship between the
Lower Party Organs and the State Administration," Slavic
Review, XXIV, 2 (June 1965), 215-40.

_____. "The Soviet System: Petrification or Pluralism?" Pro-
blems of Communism, No. 2 (March/April 1972), 25-45.

Kassof, Allen. "The Administered Society: Totalitarianism without
Terror," World Politics, XVI, 4 (July 1964), 558-75.

Landes, David. "The Industrial Revolution: 1750-1850," Chapters
in Western Civilization. Vol. II. 3rd ed. New York: Columbia
University Press, 1962.

Latham, Earl. "The Group Bases of Politics: Notes for a Theory,"
American Political Science Review, XLVI, 2 (June 1952), 376-97.

Lindblom, Charles E. "The Science of 'Muddling Through'," Public
Administration Review, XIX, 1 (Winter 1959), 79-88.

Lowi, Theodore J. "American Business, Public Policy, Case-Studies
and Political Theory," World Politics, XVI, 4 (July 1964), 676-
715.

Merelman, Richard M. "On the Neo-Elitist Critique of Community
Power," American Political Science Review, LXII, 2 (June 1968),
451-60.

Nelson, John S. "Theories of Convergence," Newsletter on the Comparative Study of Communism, 4, 2 (Feburary 1971), 11-28.

Osborn, Robert J. "Citizen versus Administration in the USSR,"
Soviet Studies, XVII, 2 (September 1965) 226-37.

_____. "The Role of Social Institutions," The Future of Communist
Society. Edited by Walter Laqueur and Leopold Labedz. New
York: Federick A. Praeger, 1962.

Osborn, Robert J. and Thomas A. Reiner. "Soviet City Planning,"
Journal of the American Institute of Planners, XXVII, 4 (November 1962), 239-49.

Powell, David E. "The Social Costs of Modernization: Ecological
Problems in the USSR," World Politics, XXLIII, 4 (July 1971),
618-34.

Schroeder, Gertrude. "Soviet Economic Reforms at an Impasse," Problems of Communism, XX, 4 (July/August 1971), 36-46.

_____. "Soviet Technology: System vs. Progress," Problems of Communism, XIX, 5 (September/October, 1970), pp. 19-29.

Sosnovy, Timothy, "Housing Conditions and Urban Development in the U.S.S.R." New Directions in the Soviet Economy, Part II-B. Joint Economic Committee Subcommittee on Foreign Economic Policy, United States Congress, 89th Congress, 2nd Session. Washington, D.C.: U.S. Government Printing Office, 1966, pp. 533-53.

_____. "The Soviet City." Dimensions of Soviet Economic Power. Joint Economic Committee, United States Congress, 87th Congress, 2nd Session. Washington, D.C.: U.S. Government Printing Office, 1963, pp. 325-45.

Stewart, Philip H. "Soviet Interest Groups and the Policy Process: The Repeal of Production Education," World Politics, XXIII, 1 (October 1969), 29-50.

Taubman, William. "The Change to Change in Communist Systems: Modernization, Post-Modernization and Soviet Politics." Paper prepared for delivery at the annual meeting of the American Political Science Association, Washington, D.C., September 1972.

WILLIAM TAUBMAN is Assistant Professor of Political Science at Amherst College. He is the author of The View From Lenin Hills: Soviet Youth in Ferment, as well as various articles on Soviet and international affairs.

Professor Taubman studied for a year at Moscow State University as a participant in the Soviet-American academic exchange program, and has travelled widely in the USSR and Eastern Europe. He has held Woodrow Wilson, Foreign Area, and Fulbright-Hays fellowships, and in 1970-71 served on the Planning and Coordination staff of the U.S. Department of State as an International Affairs Fellow of the Council on Foreign Relations.

Professor Taubman received his A.B. from Harvard College, and his M.A., Certificate of the Russian Institute, and Ph.D. from Columbia University.